LIFE *Magic*

LIFE *Magic*

The Renowned Psychic Healer
Shares Her 7 Keys
to Finding Your Power
and Living Your Purpose

LAURA BUSHNELL

miramax books

HYPERION

NEW YORK

ISBN 1-4013-5227-8

First Edition
10   9   8   7   6   5   4   3   2   1

CONTENTS

INTRODUCTION

Y ou are destined to have a magical life.

You, dear reader, are precious and have a purpose here on this earth. I wrote this book to help you uncover your purpose and accelerate your life—to move you closer to the life of your dreams.

You may be searching—searching for that mysterious "something" that feels missing from your life and leaves you feeling empty. You may not be in touch with your spirit. You may be tired of trying to control your life, or sense that something is about to happen but it never does. You may feel you don't know where you're headed, or that you're out of the flow of life. You may not even know how to listen to your heart. Or you may just simply feel stuck.

Life Magic connects you to your magical self, that part of you that knows truth, has faith in miracles, and can lead you to the life you've dreamed of having. Your magical self wants you to have fun, connect, and go forward in your life. It speaks to you through hunches, intuition, and inspired thought. The more you listen to your magical self, the faster it will guide you to your magical life—the beautiful destiny you were born to live. And the faster you get unstuck!

What is magic? When children first began to call me "the Magic Lady" many years ago, I admit that the words used to scare me, because I associated magic with witches hovering over steamy cauldrons or performers chanting "hocus pocus" and making things disappear. Since I love words, I did some research and discovered that the root meaning of *magic* is *magi*, a Persian word meaning "to bring light to." At its most fundamental level, magic is about enlightenment. Magicians date back as far as primitive societies, who celebrated and respected the individuals they considered their "enlightened ones." Magicians have been called many different names over the years: the Ancient Greeks called them "philosophers"; in England and France they were called "druids" or "bards"; the Egyptians called their magicians "priests"; and the cabalists called them "prophets."

Throughout history, the magical arts were kept a secret, and only a select group of people were given the teachings. In truth, the only real secret was how to access powers that everyone possessed—and that we all still have today. Everything you need to practice the ancient art of magic is already in your heart. The secret science is a secret no more: the Seven Keys of Life Magic will teach you to awaken the knowledge of the spirit, the most powerful knowledge you possess. And once you reclaim your personal magic, you will be able to create the magical life your heart desires.

How do you know if you are searching for your personal

magic? Listen, for a moment, to your heart. It's asking for you. Can you hear it? We all have questions: *Where am I going? What should I do? Who will I share my life with? How can I be fulfilled? How do I get healthy?* A lot of us are looking for the same answers in the same places. We examine our pasts. We look high and low for inspiration. We ask other people for advice and spend hours weighing alternatives and thinking about what we should do next. Sometimes our thoughts can lead us in circles of doubt and indecision.

We can find the answers when we look within. During almost three decades of teaching Life Magic, I have helped thousands of men and women get in touch with their personal magic and start living their dreams. I am a transformational clairvoyant; that means that I was born with the ability to see the thoughts, feelings, and energy fields that surround people, revealing their talents and tendencies and even their state of health. This gift of being able to see beyond normal sight has given me the opportunity to be of service all of my life. I have been blessed to use my gifts to help people create lives that are harmonious and graceful, and without fear and limitation.

When you discover the magic in your life, you will see the magic in every day and share this magic with others. Imagine having the ability to clear away the obstacles that once held you back. Worry and indecision will be a thing of the past, and you will be free to pursue the destiny you were born to fulfill. You'll never again lose precious time overanalyzing your options, because you'll feel confident enough to make them a reality—to start *living* the possibilities instead of just thinking about them!

Life Magic will guide you to the meaningful, peaceful, loving life you seek. I have drawn on my knowledge of ancient alchemy, ritual, and forms of focused, empowered prayer to develop my Seven Keys. They are the result of my own life experiences, my decades working with clients, and the time I spent with Mother Teresa, Elisabeth Kübler-Ross, Stephen Levine, and Ram Dass—all distilled into seven steps. I call them "keys" because they are just that: by focusing your thoughts and activating your intentions, they will unlock the doors to the life you want. These Seven Keys can help anybody change his or her life. I see it happen every day!

The people I help are probably a lot like you—interesting, creative, even successful people who want to get more out of life, or find their purpose, or just develop another way to look at their lives and understand the decisions they've made. Clients come to me for reasons you may recognize. You may want to marry, have a beautiful home, a successful career, and a healthy body. Maybe you know you want to move forward but you don't know how. Or maybe you just feel daunted by the effort you think that moving forward will require.

When people come to me with goals or challenges like these, I look for blocks in their energy that keep them from getting what they want. I show them the possibilities that exist so that they can make new and better choices for themselves. I help them discover that they can untie the psychic knots that hold them back and make the changes that they desire. And I encourage them to remember that they have a purpose that the universe is helping them find and fulfill.

Look around, and you will also see how the universe is leading you. The power to change your life is already at work. Whether you attribute it to a hunch, an impulse, or a flash of instinct, you were destined to pickup this book and I am honored. I want you to have the magical life you deserve. As you practice the Seven

Keys of Life Magic, you will discover that we are all meant to have magical lives. But before you can experience the magic, you have to get un-stuck!

Even though I have been aware of my gifts since childhood, there have been times when I was unsure of where my life was going or how it would unfold. Life has not always been easy for me. But I have always kept learning from my own life changes and from helping others move past their limitations. I am here to guide you, dear reader, every step of the way to the magical life of health, wealth, love, and perfect self-expression that you were born to have.

Have fun and let yourself be playful. The life you ordered has arrived!

A Magical Life

I was born with the gift of sight. In French the word *clairvoyant* means "clear sight," which describes my ability to see, among other things, the electrical force field of the body. What I see are voluminous essences of light that radiate from the physical body in different, beautiful colors. I also see the energy that comes in the body, like a rainbow coming into the crown of the head. I can tell a lot when I look at a person, just by looking at their energy; without even talking to them, I can see what they're about, what they're here for, what their gifts are. One thing that's clear from what I see is that we are so much bigger than we think we are. That's why you can sometimes feel people before you meet them; you know someone is coming because their energy field has gotten there before them. So what some people consider magical, I see every day. I have seen the magic that surrounds us for as long as I can remember.

Fifty years ago, a magical life would have been called supernatural. Now it is called spiritual. And in fifty more years, it will probably have a proper name based on the understanding of what really happens when you use your heart to live your life.

A magical life is one in which you let your heart, your soul, and your mind lead you into each day. Do you know how it feels to be completely *in the moment*? It's a wonderful sense of being totally connected to your life. You embrace whatever you do with no second-guessing. You're too focused to be distracted, too present to be self-conscious, too inspired by possibilities to fear limitations or worry about results. Just take a minute and imagine it.

Now imagine a life in which you live in the moment all the time. Every day is filled with light, love, and joy. You are aware of the beauty of your surroundings—the sky with its billowing clouds, the trees with their leaves and branches, the abundance that sustains you, the love that fills your relationships. You view the world with the enthusiasm of a child. You move through the day with simplicity, lightness, and ease.

Your life is already filled with magic that's just waiting to be discovered. Magic is how we understand our natural connection to the universe. We feel it more strongly as children, when our innocence and wonder are still intact and uncompromised. As we grow older, the world comes between us and our feelings of connectedness. But magic isn't just something for children. We never have to outgrow the magic deep inside us.

Sometimes this truth can be hard to see; I know because I meet many skeptical people who question whether a beautiful, peaceful, and healing world can really exist. It's understandable if you feel this way too. Every day we are bombarded with news of the world's great pain. Acts of war and terrorism, children killing and being kidnapped, the homeless, the starving, and the diseased all fill up the news these days. How could this possibly be a magical world? You might even wonder if there is a future for us here on this planet.

Of course there is a future, and you are the creator of it. You can create a meaningful, positive life with the wisdom of your heart and the power of your love—for others, for yourself, and for the world. Love is the most powerful energy that exists. The purity of your love can bring light and clarity to all areas of your life. It's what will move you forward in the journey ahead: think of love as the gas pedal that brings you closer to your dreams—and fear as the brake that stops you. We all want to pursue our dreams, but often we try to drive with the gas and the brake on at the same time. No wonder we sometimes feel stuck!

With Life Magic you can start consciously creating your life. You will find a transformative, healing energy that releases you from fear and enhances your ability to

- *trust your instincts*
- *realize your inner beauty*
- *quiet your mind*
- *open your heart*
- *find your purpose*
- *put the past behind you*
- *connect with your spirit*
- *create enlightened relationships.*

You'll also discover that life takes far less effort than before. Spirituality doesn't have to be as much hard work as people often make it out to be. You may have been taking yourself way too seriously all these years! Your magical self wants you to play, to experience happiness and joy—and it will help you do so, if you give it permission.

Consider Life Magic a guide to getting you in touch with your magical self. Make this book your companion; let it support you, advise you, inspire you to ask insightful questions about how you are living your life, and show you how to find the answers. The journey is not an intellectual voyage; as you develop your magical self, you will find more reasons to laugh and smile every day. With your focus and attention, Life Magic will clear away everything that has come between you and your magical self and bring magic and joy into your daily life.

Life Magic is about reclaiming what is natural. So before we go further, here's a simple exercise to bring you back to your natural rhythm and flow. Like everything around us, we are made up of the four elements. You can honor the elements by chanting these words out loud four times:

> *The earth*
> *The air*
> *The water*
> *The fire*
> *Return, Return, Return, Return*

Life Magic

The Seven Keys of Life Magic will show you how to create a working pattern for your life with the ancient wisdom of your heart. To unlock this wisdom, you must get your mind in sync with your heart. When your heart and your mind are working together, you are in the flow of life. You feel like you can do anything, and you feel confident in the choices you make.

As adults we often forget what it is to follow our hearts. The mind tries to assert control through expectations, fears, and doubt. The mind can be a dangerous place to be; it will keep us in the past or the future, regretting what has happened or worrying about days to come. For when we have one foot in yesterday and another in tomorrow, we cast a shadow on today, shedding darkness on the beauty of the now. In the case of my client Matthew, for example, I was able to see that the fears of his mind were overshadowing the love in his heart. Matthew went though a difficult divorce when he was forty, then met a wonderful woman named Nancy a few years later. Almost a decade after his divorce, Matthew was afraid to marry Nancy, out of fear that he would have to go through the difficulty of divorce again. Matthew was in his mind, living in the past, unable to feel the joy of the present.

A life that has meaning and gives energy to those around you is a life that is lived from the heart. Magic exists only in your heart; in fact, your mind can be so threatened by magic that it creates roadblocks that keep your magic out of reach. The Seven Keys of Life Magic eliminate those roadblocks and open the heart to shape our relationships with ourselves, with others, with the universe, and with the Divine. Each of the Seven Magic Keys addresses a different stage of that process:

> *Key One, Expect Magic, prepares you to embrace the magic that surrounds you;*
> *Key Two, Your Thoughts Are Your Prayers, teaches you how to use thoughts to release worry and manifest your dreams;*

*Key Three, "Your Heart is Your Lantern," helps you redis-
cover the ability to listen to your heart and see your
inner beauty;*

*Key Four, Your Will Is Your Wand, focuses on tapping into
the powers of the universe and developing the powers
of intention and intuition;*

*Key Five, Your Words Are Your Invocations, reveals how
to harness the awesome power of words to create your
reality;*

*Key Six, You Must Ask in Order to Receive, puts you in
touch with the spririt world and your angels;*

*Key Seven, Share the Magic, shows you how to connect
and celebrate with others.*

Each of the following chapters introduces you to one of the magic keys. You will find exercises that will give you personal experience of each key, providing firsthand knowledge of its possible applications to your life. But they only work if you do them! And why wouldn't you want to? They're fun, and they will prepare you for the 7 Keys that follow. Ideas discussed in the earlier chapters are invoked in the subsequent ones, so you'll get the best results if you read the chapters in order and experience the full benefit of the alchemical effect that develops as they build on each other.

You will also read stories of how these keys have changed the lives of other men and women like yourself. The rapid progress I've seen in my clients' lives has demonstrated time and again the power of these keys to accelerate their progress toward their life's purpose. They have worked for the people I've helped, and I am positive that they'll work for you too.

It is important to keep in mind that my clients achieve their healing through their own magic, not mine. My psychic gifts do play a role, to be sure; I instinctively see what my clients are feeling or creating in their lives, and how long it will take to manifest. I use my gifts to help clients get to the core of what they really want, so they can do the work of opening their hearts and moving forward with their lives. My words just help them recognize the answers they already have deep inside—and can finally listen to once they find their own magic.

In other words, you don't have to be a clairvoyant to benefit from Life Magic. Nor do you need to see a clairvoyant to gain from the wisdom in the chapters that follow. I'm really just like you—I've only learned how to listen and trust my magic, just as you will learn to listen and trust your own.

Think of Life Magic as a ladder to your higher consciousness. After you have used the ladder to reach a higher plane of understanding, you won't need it any longer. There's no need to cling to my magic. It's your magic that will change your life; you must simply learn to trust in it. The first key, Expect Magic, will get you started.

Exercise Your Spirit:	Your Magic Notebook
What you will need:	A notebook and pen
Time:	15 minutes or as long as you want

To prepare for the first key, I recommend that you begin a journal—your own magic notebook, where you can write about your experiences and keep track of your progress. Journaling your experience will help you find what is natural again. You will start to notice more magical moments as you develop your magic, so write them down as you experience them.

Whenever you read a new exercise, use your magic notebook to make comments or schedule your next time to practice. I suggest that you set time aside at least once a week to practice these exercises. My most dedicated clients have practiced these exercises consistently, even daily, and they have rapidly created wonderful changes in their lives as a result.

The first key is about expecting magic. Before you read further, just take a moment to write in your journal anything that happened to you today that fits your idea of magic. Don't think too hard about it. Remember, this is meant to be fun!

Here's a fun and simple way to start out the first day of your magical journey smiling inside and out:

Exercise Your Spirit:	**Morning Smiles**
What you will need:	**You**
Time:	**5 minutes**

Before you get out of bed tomorrow morning, spend five minutes with your eyes closed and allow all of your organs to smile. Just imagine what each organ would feel like if it were smiling. You'll be smiling when you get out of bed!

CHAPTER 1

KEY 1: Expect Magic

There are only two ways to live your life.
One is as though nothing is a miracle.
The other one is as though everything is a miracle.

—ALBERT EINSTEIN

If you expect magic, something magical will happen. When you believe in magic, there is a true enthusiasm to your life. You believe anything is possible—because it is! You regain the optimism and exuberance you had as a young child. You can see the magic around you, because you're no longer distracted by worry and fear.

The Italian movie director Federico Fellini once said, "Never lose your childlike enthusiasm and things will come your way." Think about how children view the world. They pay no attention to limits. They don't sit around worrying if they're good enough or if they have enough. Instead, they revel in the moment, in the endless possibilities of the now, fearless and full of life. They are open to the magic that surrounds them.

Have you ever seen a child playing in a park? Would you ever ask a child, "Why are you playing? What are you going to get from it? What is your purpose in playing?" Children just enjoy the energy. But as we become adults, we begin to think only about the future, and gradually our minds take over and deny us the magic we saw in childhood. We go from seeing magic everywhere to forgetting how to recognize it. But it's never too late to reclaim that innocent interest in the unknown. The first step is to expect magic, to believe in the possibility of unseen forces in the universe. Once you allow yourself to begin expecting it, you'll soon start seeing magic all the time.

Exercise Your Spirit:	**The White Candle**
What you will need:	**One white candle**
Time:	**10 minutes**

- *Find a quiet, private place. You are going to give yourself ten minutes to relax and become again like a child. For example, remember when you were five years old and it was your birthday? You had a birthday cake placed right in front of you and you got to make one huge wish! This exercise is just like that.*
- *Light your white candle.*
- *Say these words, out loud, three times:*

  Clear the path. Clear my way.
  Help me see magic every day.

- *Close your eyes and visualize yourself really happy.*
- *Open your eyes and breathe into your heart, as you watch the candle burn.*
- *Make one wish and hold the thought.*

- *Blow out the candle, just as you did when you were a child.*
- *Clap your hands three times.*
- *And don't tell anyone your wish!*
- *Take a walk, do some physical exercise, do household chores, or have something to eat.*

You Create What You Expect

My client Sue Yang Eaves came to me lost and forlorn after having to close down her four-year-old clothing manufacturing business. At the age of thirty-three, she had a young daughter and a wonderful husband who worked with her, but she felt like a failure. When she voiced her concerns about losing her home and not paying her bills, we spoke about the laws of expectation. I told her that something better was right over her head. I explained that when one door closes, another is waiting to open—but if you do not expect another door, your eyes will never see it open. Sue immediately understood the role that her expectations would play as she moved forward; she was so uplifted when she left that day that an idea for a clothing design came to her. Sue had stopped by a used clothing store to search for vintage clothes when she spotted a beautiful antique scarf. She picked it up and held it up over her white T-shirt and was hit with a brainstorm. She had a vision for a design. She went right to work making it from some scraps and within two weeks had sold it to a major department store!

Sue came back to see me shortly after she had received her first department store order, but this time she was full of fear. Excitement also brings a certain kind of fear with it. Sue was afraid to get "too excited" because she was expecting failure. She was pulling her energy down and repressing it. I encouraged her to feel the excitement and to allow it to move into her body. Excitement is a very sensual and passionate energy; it creates momentum and makes you feel alive. Sue learned to use this energy to attract many new accounts, and she now has her special designs all over the country and sees clothes from her line, Duo Originals, in many fashion magazines. Losing her home is the last thing on her mind!

Let's talk for a moment about expectations. When was the last time you were really surprised? How often have you imagined a possible scenario that then came true? Have you ever envisioned a goal that you then successfully pursued?

Most of the time, we create what we expect. Because you are the creator of your own life, a lot of the time when you think it, you live it. For example, we often think negative thoughts about ourselves; by doing so, we create our own negative environment and manifest our negativity. Fortunately, the same is true with our positive thoughts. We'll explore what to do with that power in later keys, and when you learn how to harness it, you'll be amazed at the results you can create.

A lot of us don't even realize we have this power, however. You don't have to recognize the power to be under its influence. It may be invisible to you, even as you use it all the time. For example, if we have been hurt in the past, we often come to expect that we will be hurt again. We feel it, we predict it: we may even attract it. At the same time, we fear it. And it's this fear that comes between us and our destiny, keeping us from moving forward, and hiding our magic from our view.

Fear is a creation of the mind, not of the heart. Like other creations of the mind, fear may feel natural, but it's not. In fact, it's a sign that we've lost touch with what is natural. Fear is only here to serve as a brake and help us turn a corner or make a change—not to stop us in our tracks. Listen to what it is trying to tell you. What are you afraid of?

The universe wants you to find your natural flow. As we grow older and our mind comes between us and our magic, we may go longer and longer without any interaction with our elemental self. We may do so many unnatural things over the years that we can even forget what is natural, or lose sight of the natural order of the universe that is here to support us.

We can start to restore that order, and quiet the role of fear in our life, by deciding to let magic in. Expecting magic is an expectation of the heart, though you need the mind to cooperate. Of course, it takes some practice to keep the mind from getting in the way. Often the magical self will start you going on something and then the mind gets involved. When my client Jill first started to study massage, she could tell right away that she felt completely natural doing it. Her spirit told her that on some level she knew what to do: she just naturally knew where to touch and how to help others. But then her mind started filling her with doubt, telling her she couldn't know as much as her spirit was telling her she did, because she had just started the program and hadn't studied enough or read enough of the books. Fortunately, she kept going, and now she's teaching her special techniques at a massage school. Remember, the mind can't experience magic, so it makes a decision about what you're doing and puts an expectation on it that really stops the magical self.

When we expect magic, we start to get the mind to stay out of the way. The mind wants evidence that magic exists. Of course, this evidence is everywhere! But the mind doesn't see it that way, at least not at first. By introducing the mind to the possibility of magic, we begin taking some of the power of the mind and reclaiming it for the heart. That's why it's so important to expect magic—so you can more clearly manifest it, and then recognize it as magic when you do.

Tom, a forty-two-year-old accountant, came to see me after watching his girlfriend complete the magic keys and create the acting career she had always wanted. He had never even imagined seeing someone like me, and he arrived skeptical but curious—skeptically curious, for certain! He dreaded going to his accounting job every day because his real interest was photography. That is what drove him to take the chance of seeing me. Once he decided to come, he began to notice how nervous he became: he was afraid of change. As soon as I began to talk about his creativity, he started to cry, and he grew ever more emotional as he worked with the Seven Keys. It was a homecoming he will never forget.

Tom had stopped listening to his heart for so long that he had given up hope and was no longer open to the universe's messages. I asked him to follow his hunches to get in touch with the magic that surrounded him. One day he woke up with the normal desire for a cup of coffee but discovered he had run out of coffee beans. As he was pulling into a parking place at Starbucks later that morning, another car took his spot. But instead of getting angry as he normally would, he remembered to be on the lookout for magic and decided it was not where he was meant to go. He went to a second coffee shop, where he was sitting outside when a man came up with a little Lab puppy. The men started a conversation, and it turned out they had gone to the same college in another part of the country. The man with the puppy was an agent for photographers who was looking for a photographer for a film project. They became friends, and soon Tom found himself in a new photography career looking forward to going to work every day!

Down the line, you'll have to assure the mind that the inspiration that comes from magic will bring more of what you want and enjoy into your life. For now, however, you can start by noticing and celebrating all the magic that you see.

Exercise Your Spirit:	Expect Magic
What you will need:	One piece of paper and a green pen
Time:	Ongoing

- *Write in big green letters on a piece of typing paper, "Something magical is about to happen!"*
- *Place it wherever you look when you wake up in the morning.*
- *Pay attention to what you notice once you start expecting magic. The green writing is like a green light. Go!*

Give Yourself Permission

Once you start expecting magic and seeing it everywhere, you'll begin noticing little indicators that will help you confirm that you are on the right path. These are moments of alignment or synchronicity that you may have previously dismissed as coincidences.

The more magic you see, however, the more clearly you recognize that everything in your life is in its own perfect place.

Your mind is used to dismissing coincidences as random, chance occurrences, but there's nothing random about them. We are the creator of everything that happens in our life, and everything is perfect, whether we realize it or not. When we're not in touch with our magic, we may not truly believe that such perfection exists. But our magical selves are always trying to reach us and teach us. Coincidences are those moments when your magical self is speaking to you.

Your magical self knows your destiny and knows that you deserve more joy and abundance than the mind believes you can have. Sometimes that's hard to accept. My upbringing did not teach me that I was worthy of the life I have created. I used my keys to create a wonderful family, health, and a meaningful career. I had to follow my heart all the way here, and you can too. So often I've seen people struggling to feel worthy of the happiness their magical self has in store for them. They tell me it all seems too good to be true. Think about that phrase; you've heard it a million times. But have you ever heard that something is too *bad* to be true? Of course not; if it's bad, we naturally believe it! What's at the heart of believing that things can't be true when they're good? Fear—the familiar expectation of the mind. Don't believe it! Instead, try playing with these words: *It's just good enough to be true—and it's getting better all the time!*

If the mind has convinced us to expect the worst, we may have trouble accepting that the best is waiting for us, even when it is right in front of our eyes. I was not expecting to fall in love again. My lover had died of lung cancer, and when I met my husband, I was not expecting to meet anyone. He was right in front of me trying to get my attention, and he would not take no for an answer! He knew what he wanted and how he felt about me. You too have to give yourself permission to live the life you desire. Every cell and molecule is programmed to lead us to our destiny, but we won't get anywhere if we don't feel worthy of the destination. No matter how clearly it's laid out for us, we won't claim it until we tell ourselves that it's okay to do so—that we love ourselves enough to deserve it. When you give yourself permission, you take your foot off the brake and put it on that gas pedal of love, and you start moving forward toward the life you have always deserved.

Magic Calling

Once you accept that you deserve to be here for a reason, your magical self will intensify its efforts to make you see what that reason is. Your magic is closely linked with your calling, the role you are here in this world to play. The more magic you expect, the more prepared you'll be to recognize your calling when it presents itself to you. Don't worry about missing it; if you don't hear the whispers, the universe will turn up the volume.

How will you know if you are doing what you are meant to do? Sometimes a calling comes as a dream, sometimes as a voice, or sometimes as the simple knowledge of what you want to do. We've all seen children who announce they will be doctors when they grow up, and then we watch them go to medical school and follow their calling into adulthood. On the other hand, we've also witnessed bright, talented people who always seem lost, unable to trust their instincts and follow a single path.

Only you will know when your calling comes to you. One word of wisdom: don't insist on a trumpet, because sometimes the answers are heard in silence. As you work with the remaining six keys, you will develop your intuitive abilities that will help you find your calling. Expect to see the signs among the moments of magic you observe. And don't worry if it takes a while to find your path. I, for one, didn't discover for many years how to bring to fulfillment the gifts I knew I possessed, even though they made me aware of the magic that surrounds us all. It took some time and experience for me to develop into who I am today.

Long before I was born, a fortune-teller at a county fair in Idaho told my mother that she would have a daughter with the gift of sight. I wasn't very old before it became clear that the prophecy had come true. I was eight years old when a vision of the death of my friend's father came to me in the middle of a card game. We were playing go fish when I went into a trance and said, "I'm sorry, Brenda . . . your father's going to die. Go tell him that you love him." The next morning we awoke to sirens. Brenda's father had died of a heart attack.

Luckily not all of the visions I received turned out to be so troubling, and my gifts provided the entertainment at many a slumber party as I was growing up. Though I had dreams of growing up and becoming a journalist, I began a grassroots clairvoyance practice as a teenager because my schoolmates and friends would always ask me to do a "reading" for them. Without knowing that it was my calling to do so, I had already established the pattern of my life—guiding people to greater clarity and hope.

It wasn't until I was a young woman in my twenties that I was called into my destiny. I had a very comfortable life, but I was not giving full expression to my gifts. In my heart, I knew something was missing; I knew there was more for me to do. Finally, after a series of signs and coincidences too unmistakable for me to deny, I was compelled to abandon my comfortable life and set out on my path. While some of the signs were intense, others were pretty subtle—as fleeting as the scent of roses, as seemingly random as strangers whose paths briefly crossed my own—but I knew enough to look for them and recognize them when they appeared. I also knew enough not to turn away and deny myself the joy of living my destiny despite all the sacrifices that were asked of me. The word *sacrifice*, at its roots, means, "to make holy." What better to lead me to my destiny? It was all part of my journey.

The most compelling and supportive reminders of my calling have been the apparitions of the Virgin Mary that have visited me since the age of five. There was no religious practice in my family when I was growing up, but when a hired man on our farm left behind a picture of Jesus, I put it in a closet where I would go to pray. I was a little five-year-old girl, praying in that closet, when one day I was overcome by a soothing presence as a big ball of light appeared before me. The Virgin Mary materialized in holographic form, and her heart opened into a rose. As my own heart started to burn, the rose blooming from her heart showered its petals on the earth, and as each petal landed on the closet floor, it magically turned into another rose.

Over the years these visions have been ongoing, and it was a vivid and beautiful vision of the Holy Mother that inspired me to commit myself to my life's work as a young woman. The Virgin communicates with me through thought transference and imagery, giving meaning and purpose to my gifts. I know that she represents a universal female consciousness that is helping many to love and nurture life. Everything I do is energized and guided by my connection and devotion to her. She has led me to the place of being able to help other people, as have the spiritual leaders I have known and the clients I have worked with, each and every one of whom I count among my teachers.

Since devoting my life to the pursuit of my calling, I have worked in almost every aspect of the psychic world: from tarot cards, palm reading, and astrology to healing animals and removing spirits from homes; from communicating with the deceased to past life regression and even psychic surgery. To give my clients additional tools to achieve their life dreams, I've developed a series of Magic Lady programs on compact disc that use consciously structured visualization to help achieve amazing results in 108 days in the areas of relationships, work, abundance, and healing. It is all as natural as breathing to me. Today I live in Los Angeles, where I often work with a Hollywood clientele, including actors, directors, and producers; because of my ability to keep movie sets energetically balanced, I have found myself involved with some of the largest-grossing movies ever produced, though confidentiality agreements prevent me from mentioning their names.

Could I have possibly expected this life as a little girl growing up on a small farm in Idaho? Yes! I expected to have an interesting and exciting life, and I have created it by listening to spirit and doing what is natural—my true work.

As with all magic, finding your true work is something that you need to give focused and loving attention to. You must learn both how to dream and how to act upon your dream. And once you take action, you must maintain the dream, no matter what. This will become easier and more natural as you work with the rest of the magic keys. Soon you will recognize that you are a powerful being with the entire world at your fingertips!

Don't worry if you do not know your calling right now; you will find it when the time is right. What is important is that you don't lose sight of the fact that you too have gifts waiting to be shared with the world. In fact, the world is waiting for you to share them. So it is worth trying to find out whether you have yet begun doing what you are meant to do.

See if any of the below statements describe your work life:

I miss work a lot because of illness.
I can't wait for weekends.
I often compare my level of success to the success of others.
If I had enough money, I would retire tomorrow.
I just don't feel that I can make things happen.
I don't feel creative.
I don't like or identify with the people I am working with.
I change jobs so often that people can't keep track of me.

If any of these resonate with you, you probably haven't found your life's true work yet. But look for the clues in the magic you see. Expect guidance, and it will come! My client Betty agreed with many of those statements; then she began using her magic and asking for clues. As a result, she was ready when opportunity presented itself one day when she was out shopping. Betty was just looking for a new outfit when the sales clerk asked her if she could help out a woman from out of town who was shopping in the same store. The woman had noticed her and liked her style, and now Betty has a very exciting career as a stylist to the stars. Without ever handing out a resume, Betty created a job that fits her perfectly, and she's getting paid to do what she naturally does well!

When you do find your path, your journey will become notice-ably more enjoyable. You will feel more and more relaxed and will discover beauty in things that you had never before conceived of as being beautiful. You will look at your world differently, as though it were brighter or clearer. The smallest things will start having significance. You will find that life is a blessing and a gift. The world will grow more mysterious, but you won't worry about feeling less knowledgeable: you'll celebrate your feelings of innocence.

This is not to say that there will not be challenges, but you will respond to them in a completely different way, looking for the messages that each challenge can provide. You will be able to navigate through life with greater ease. Many of my clients report back to me that they are surprised at the lack of fear and hesitation in their lives once they use the Seven Keys.

My client Corey Powell is a very gifted hairstylist, a true artist who loves what he does. Corey started a hair salon together with his boyfriend, who was the business brains of the operation, and they seemed to be headed for a tremendous success. But when Corey and his boyfriend broke up, Corey was afraid he couldn't run the salon on his own. That's when he came to me—eager to reach for the stars but worried that his artistic temperament couldn't provide the business know-how that his boyfriend had offered. We began working the Seven Keys, and soon Corey was moving beyond his setback to take charge of his life and his salon. He built his business and now does hair for Cameron Diaz, Reese Witherspoon, and Kim Basinger, to name just a few. He treats everyone with the same love and excitement and still approaches his work as a form of art, and he's able to run his business with the confidence and ability he initially feared he would never have. He rose to the challenge of his boyfriend's departure, and now he's in a better position than he dreamed he would be.

Say Yes to You

It is your time now. As you search for your destiny, you need to make sure that it's *your* destiny that you claim. So many times I find that my clients sabotage their own dreams by listening to others. Family and friends will say things such as "You can't do that!" "You're too old!" "That's too big of a risk!" or "There is no money in that!" You don't have to hear too much of such talk before your dream is completely stifled.

Certainly, there are times when we need to listen to others and factor in what they say, but there are also times when listening to ourselves is paramount. In order to ignite the magic, you must be an individual, free from outside influences, prepared to set boundaries and separate yourself from others. This often requires learning how to say no—because sometimes saying no to others is saying yes to you.

Take Maggie, for instance. She was thirty-seven when she was laid off from her high-powered management job. While Maggie was disappointed to lose her six-figure income, life in a corporation had never been her dream. Maggie had spent her life wanting to be a singer, but her mother had long ago told her to study business, because music was "not a career." She followed her mother's advice and became a business executive, so it was no surprise that she lost her job, because it was not what her spirit was longing to do.

Maggie decided it was time to do something completely different, so she studied to become a personal trainer—until her brother nosed his way into her business and told her that this was "not a career" either. Listening to her brother, Maggie ended her personal training stint and became a facialist—something she loved because she had beautiful skin and enjoyed helping others take care of theirs. Maggie soon found herself happy in this new career, but her friends and family harangued her that she would never be financially secure if she were "just a facialist." So Maggie was struggling, even though she loved her newfound work. Her family did nothing but fan the flames of her anxiety, and soon she was mired in worry about *everything*—money, the "right" career, love, and her life's path.

Most painful of all were Maggie's mother's words before she died, when she told Maggie, "You really should have studied voice, because you would have been a wonderful recording artist!" In disbelief that her mother had reversed course, Maggie began to question whether or not she should start singing—years after she had abandoned the dream.

When Maggie contacted me to sort all these things out, shortly after her mother's death, she was considering yet another career change, this time to study ultrasound. Though the two-year program cost $25,000, she felt that getting this certification would yield more financial security. Her brother told her that she would not be good at this and she should not even try, revealing that he simply didn't think Maggie was good with the sciences! Maggie was confused, afraid that she would never be able to do anything right according to her family. No wonder: with every choice Maggie made, her family responded with another negative voice.

By this point Maggie had lost all access to her inner soul voice. Her magic was lost under layers of fear and doubt—fear which Maggie's family and friends had repeatedly given to her (and which she repeatedly accepted). This accomplished, educated, and successful woman was so trapped in fear that she was reduced to grasping for something to fall back on. As her loneliness mounted, she began to see the ultrasound course as a chance to meet a doctor. Certainly it was a possibility, but so was meeting a doctor at the grocery store—which would save her $25,000 and two precious years of her life!

I suggested that Maggie give my life magic keys a try and not discuss anything with her family until she had worked the Seven Keys. Within two months, she came to the breakthrough realization that she had never believed in herself. She was so busy trying to get others' approval that she had left herself out of the equation. Once she began to put herself into her facial business full time, Maggie created a very strong, stable life career for herself. She is already developing new products, and now her brother is seeking her advice on his business affairs!

The takeaway here is, as stated in the Bible, "Do not cast your pearls before swine." In other words, do not share your dreams with those who do not understand them. As you are finding your life path, you should keep your work secret. We have been trained throughout our lives to listen to others, but it's important that you learn to listen to your individual, private inner voice. Your magical self needs to live its own dreams; it cannot live with other people's fear. As Dr. Carl Jung said, "there is no better means of intensifying the treasured feeling of individuality, than the possession of a secret which the individual has pledged to guard." That's why the wish you made with the white candle is a secret!

Other people will often try to inflict their fear on you; chances are, someone has recently tried. Does anybody come to mind? Did you let them "gift" you with their fear? Did you realize they were doing it? More important, will you realize it next time, and stop them before they can pass it on to you?

To find your destiny, you must be true to yourself. The magic keys that follow will help you do so, by supporting your efforts to master the four things necessary for being true to yourself:

1. *Remain in the present: Keys Two and Five will teach you to quiet your mind and focus your prayers, which will help you stay out of the past and the future and firmly planted in the now.*
2. *Never mask your feelings: The exercises in Key Three will open your heart so you can understand the feelings that express the truth of who you are.*
3. *Never listen to anybody's idea of who you are: Key Four will help you strengthen your ability to trust yourself and the world around you.*
4. *Be the co-creator of your own reality: Keys Six and Seven offer the strength and power to live your own life and to share it with others.*

Celebrate You and Celebrate Your Life Now!

One of the ways you can assert your individuality is to do things you love to do. Unfortunately, many of us put off the things we love to do and dwell on the things we think we *have* to do. Most people do not even know what they really love to do. It is perhaps time to be a little more spontaneous. When was the last time you went out in some fresh snow and made an angel with your arms and legs? When was the last time you saw a rainbow and really stopped to look at it? Guess what: it is time to start! The next exercise will help you create the time to be yourself and to find out what you like to do.

Exercise Your Spirit:	Your Future in the Present
What you will need:	A notebook and pen
Time:	15 minutes or as long as you want

- *In your magic notebook, make a list of three fun activities that you have been wanting to do in your life, including simple activities that you may have been putting off. This is not meant to be an intensive, deep self-analysis—just a chance to add some fun and adventure to your life. You may want to do something that you previously rejected because it just was "not you." Begin with something simple yet significant, something you can do on your own—like writing a poem. Then learn a skill of some kind, like typing or cooking. Doing new things transforms your sense of who you are and increases your self-respect.*
- *Pick at least one of these activities and map out the necessary measures to begin it as soon as possible.*
- *Go to your calendar to schedule it and make it a regular part of your life.*
- *Establish a future check-in date (in about six weeks) for you to come back and ask yourself if you enjoyed the activity and want to continue.*
- *It's OK if you don't immediately enjoy it. Keep going! Your heart will lead you to what you really love.*

Make Plans to Move Forward

The only way to move forward, now that you are expecting magic, is to surrender to your magical self. The changes that are ahead of you are all about living from the wisdom of your heart. But in order to feel how loved you are, you must learn to quiet your mind. The next key will unlock the power of your mind.

CHAPTER **2**

KEY **2:** Your Thoughts Are Your Prayers

You can get help from teachers, but you are going to have to learn a lot by yourself, sitting alone in a room.

—DR. SEUSS

If you watch closely enough, you will begin to notice that your thoughts are actually creating your life. Every day of your life, every time you think of something, you pray for that thought to manifest itself. Your thoughts become your prayers. A prayer is actually an earnest request for something, a concentrated energy pattern that has direction and purpose. You may not realize it, but you are constantly making requests with your thoughts. You are spinning and weaving a magical world around yourself.

When you recognize the power of your thoughts, you can turn them to your good. Your thoughts can either help you or hold you back. Every day, you create your own reality by choosing how you think. There is always both a positive and a negative way of looking at life; you can see it for all its beauty and abundance, or you can see sparseness and lack. You can use your mind as either a tool or a

weapon: it is up to you to decide. You create peace or drama in your
life with your mere thoughts!

A very talented architect in his early forties, Michael was constantly questioning his ability to buy a home, despite the fact that
his accountant had been telling him he needed to do so for years.
Michael had plenty of money in the bank but he always felt poor,
because his parents had lost everything when he was ten years
old. When Michael began to use the Seven Keys, he learned to allow himself to see his abundance and to give himself permission
to enjoy it. He has since purchased his dream home; many a dinner party invitation from him has arrived in my mailbox. He
merely had to stop his mind from living in the past and thinking
thoughts of lack.

To have a magical life, you must think positive or life-enhanc-
ing thoughts. The more awareness you have about your thinking,
the easier it will be to quiet your mind and train your thinking to
serve your life, rather than keeping you stuck. This key will teach
you how to achieve a balance between your mind and your
heart—both of them existing like a figure eight in infinity, feeding
each other and working together to create the life you want.

The mind represents the air element inside of you. The voice
of the wind is the motion of human affairs. Thoughts, opinions,
values are like the winds: they rise, shift, fall back, and veer away;
they prevail for a time, freshen into gales, only to die again. The
east wind belongs to new ventures and blesses ambition with energy; call it up for courage, patience, and clarity. The south wind
favors love, imagination, and fulfillment; use it in love enchant-
ments and to achieve harmony in close relationships. The west
wind erases doubt, guilt, fear, envy, and hate; it will renew confidence and restore hope. The north wind brings with it wisdom

and transcends the other winds as a source of spiritual strength; it will protect you and increase intuition and divinatory power. Join me in asking the winds to be part of our journey:

Exercise Your Spirit: **Air Blessing**
What you will need: **You**
Time: **5–10 minutes**

- *Breathe deeply seven times and say these words aloud:*

> *Oh, great Air, please bring me home,*
> *Let me feel you in my bones.*

> *Sing your songs out through my breath,*
> *Laugh and sing until my death.*

> *Oh, great Air, please clear my thoughts.*
> *Your great knowledge can't be bought.*

> *Blow me to new places in my mind.*
> *Please, dear Air be warm and kind.*

- *Burn some incense. Smell a flower. Listen to the wind. Feel the air around you and give thanks.*

My gift of sight has given me the opportunity to learn how our thoughts and our minds operate. Ever since childhood, I have had the ability to see thoughts. I can see their color and shape as they radiate out from each of us, whether they are spoken or not. As a child, I would sit in front of the mirror and watch the changes that took place in my energy field when I thought certain thoughts. Later, as I worked with clients, I noticed that similar changes occurred when they were discussing ideas, thoughts, or emotions. I learned that every thought in the mental sphere has its own special form and vibration, and thoughts often form patterns that repeat themselves. Most important, I observed firsthand that we are all broadcasting all of our thoughts all the time—even before we say them.

All thoughts are energy. When you have a thought, it sends out an electrical current that is broadcast from your body like a radio signal. So every time you think of something, it has an effect. If you ask the universe, the universe will provide; whatever you focus on will become your reality. A quick way of recognizing that this principle is true is to think of a certain car you would someday love to own. You will naturally start noticing that model of car on the street, in the magazines you read, even on billboards and in television advertisements. Soon, everywhere you turn, you will see that car. Your broadcasting station will be calling it in!

When we don't like a song on the radio, we don't think twice about changing the station. But when it comes to our thoughts, we often leave them right where they are, even though they are not sweet music to our ears. Why do we do that? Simply because we have done it so many times that we automatically tap into those thoughts without even knowing it. That is why we sometimes don't receive what we want: we don't even realize that we're asking for something else entirely.

When you repeat a thought about yourself over and over, you are literally praying that your thought will be manifested. For instance, when you think about what you don't have, you are sending the universe the message that you are deficient. If you continue this line of thinking, then the universe will give you deficiency in return, and you probably won't get whatever you think you're lacking. I am not talking philosophy here. This goes back to the simple laws of physics: what goes up must come down, and what goes out must come back. A negative thought gets a negative response. I've seen it happen again and again.

Sandra came to me weighing herself down with questions about a relationship. She wanted to know if her partner still loved her, or whether there was anything she could do to make him love her again. She was obsessed, blaming herself and unable to stop thinking about him, and she was creating a depression with these thoughts. We went to work with the Seven Keys and began to change her thoughts from negative to positive. Sandra's questions were keeping her in her mind. Once her mind was quiet, she began to realize that the relationship was not what she really needed, she was merely afraid of being alone. She had become a beggar for love. Sandra began focusing on the solution instead of the problem, thinking about what she wanted instead of what she did not want! Six months later she was promoted at work and began dating a very kind, generous man who gave love willingly.

Fortunately, a positive thought naturally gets a positive response. So if you stop thinking about what you don't have, and instead think about how blessed you are, the universe will send even more blessings in return. Your choice really is that simple. Just send out the good and watch it come right back!

For example, if your thinking about your work goes something like this—*I hate my job, and I am never going to find my life's true work*—then anyone who is connected with your life's true work will steer clear of you, because they won't resonate with you. But if you reverse this limiting way of thinking and project a more expansive, positive expectation—*I am ready for my life's work to be revealed to me*—then you will be in harmony and will soon start manifesting your path. It defies the laws of physics to receive anything other than what you send out to the universe. This is why you will never be able to receive what you truly want if you are thinking negative thoughts.

Exercise Your Spirit: **The Sky Is Your Mirror**
What you will need: **You**
Time: **Ongoing**

- *Think of the sky as a mirror.*
- *Every time you think a thought, imagine that the thought is immediately being written in big letters with red lipstick on a huge mirror, hanging above you for the world to see.*
- *Close your eyes and think a positive thought about yourself.*
- *Now see the thought being written in red lipstick on the mirror.*

Your mirror always reflects to the world who you are and what you believe about yourself, as well as your ability to receive. If you think, I am beautiful and deserve to have it all! then those words will be written on the mirror of the sky. The more times you write it on your mirror, the more your life will reflect it and you will have a life of abundance—all from repeating this thought. Remember, energy follows thought!

The mind is a tremendous gift, and one that we should cherish; after all, the mind is here to serve our hearts. Most people, however, set limits to what the mind can do. It is the nature of the mind to seek separation instead of connection. The mind is our accumulated discontent, the storage place of our past unhappiness. The mind can never really be happy. It seeks and pursues. It compares. It obsesses. It complains. For the mind, nothing is ever enough. And even if it is "enough," the mind then becomes busy thinking into the past or the future. The now disappears and the gifts of today are gone. Often we can't see happiness and opportunity right before our very eyes, because the mind judges what's before us instead of accepting and enjoying it. Many people are living *in the mind*, searching for happiness, even when it is already here, surrounding us like the fragrance of a flower.

Have you ever heard anyone say, "I love you with all of my mind"? Of course not! They say, "I love you with all of my heart and soul." This is because no one can love from the mind. Your mind cannot *feel* the rush of a first kiss. Your mind cannot *feel* the joy of holding a child for the first time. Your mind cannot *feel* the hope of a dream about to be realized. Instead, your mind compares, processes, and focuses on the past and the future, and by doing this, it keeps you alone.

On the other hand, when you are *in the heart*, you are part of life. You are connected. This is probably the feeling that we all crave the most—to feel that we are in the flow of life, connected with another person or with the universe itself. It is only when you are in your magic that you are available to be loved, and it is only when you're in your heart that you're in your magic.

Habits of the Mind

It's easy to understand why we have come to rely so much on our minds. From an early age we are taught to analyze and think things through. Since children's minds have a tendency to roam and dream, our culture places an emphasis on teaching the mind to focus and concentrate, and it promotes these skills as the best path to success. It's no surprise that our minds became dominant as a result.

I am not saying that this early conditioning was wrong or that using our minds is somehow bad. Nothing could be further from the truth. I just want to encourage you to use your mind in ways that serve you and quicken your growth. First and foremost, I want you to use your mind to its greatest ability. Your mind loves to be exercised and expanded: it really does! Your mind can serve you with inspired thinking, creativity, imagination, and more. But the untrained mind is held back by all the negative thoughts that are clamoring about inside. Until you learn to quiet the mind and listen to your heart, the mind can't give you the best it has to offer.

When clients first come to see me, they are most often living in their minds and questioning their lives. All of us do it. We weigh ourselves down with questions: *Why doesn't he love me anymore? Why did my boss promote my colleague over me? What is my real work to be?* We spend vast amounts of time developing theories or searching for the right words that will explain away our unhappiness. But all that thinking, blaming, and judging ourselves can prevent us from experiencing life as it really is. Thinking takes so much energy and keeps us from our magical self. How can a whisper of truth or understanding find its way in when there is already such noise and disharmony going on in the mind?

When we are stuck in the mind, it's easy to get caught up in analyzing things, viewing them in a positive or negative way. The mind has been taught to operate in a mode of fear and anticipation, so it loves to have problems to analyze. But why waste your precious time analyzing? After all, there are no mistakes or accidents in life, so there's no need to evaluate everything as positive or negative. Every problem has a solution, but you rarely find it by holding on to a problem and going over and over it in your mind. More often, this is where the real trouble occurs, as you become trapped in an ongoing cycle, crippled by the limitations your thoughts place upon you. Instead, you must release the problem and allow yourself to receive the solution.

Exercise Your Spirit:	**Dynamite**
What you will need:	**Your magic notebook**
Time:	**10 minutes**

- *Think of something happening in your life right now that you are concerned or worried about.*
- *Think about it from start to finish.*
- *Think of all the possible outcomes, but most importantly, the "worst thing that could happen" scenario.*
- *Now, in your imagination, focus only on the "worst thing that could happen" scenario.*
- *Put some dynamite into this vision and blow it up!*

- *Now change the scene and envision the scenario that ends in a way that most brings peace and growth to all who are involved.*
- *Lastly, see yourself at peace.*
- *Now pinch your thumb on your left hand.*
- *Throughout the week, when you find yourself thinking "fear" or the "worst thing that could happen" thoughts, pinch your left thumb again to trigger your memory to recall the outcome that you want— the one that ends with peace, love, and growth. Fear, be gone!*

Performing this simple and easy exercise will help you to break old thinking habits that you may have collected in your life. But remember, you must always be careful of what you wish for, because you will probably get it . . . eventually. Be sure it is something you really want!

Some people love their problems so much that they don't want to lose them. I've even heard people arguing to keep their problems! They wonder how life could really go on without something to worry about, or how they would fill up the time with their friends without a problem to hash out. Many have become so conditioned to navigating a life full of problems that they will create new problems if they can't hang on to the problems they already have. But these old problems that we go over and over and over are like fish left in a refrigerator: they're still there whenever you open the door, and if you leave them there long enough, they start to stink!

My client Jane first came to see me because her marriage was on the rocks. Four years married at the age of thirty-five, Jane believed that the sole reason for her marital strife was that her husband did not understand her. Most of our first session together was spent with Jane's listing all the ways in which her husband did not know what she needed or wanted. He didn't do this, or he didn't know that. The list reading took almost an entire hour. Jane had obviously given it a lot of thought.

Before Jane left, she asked me if she could pay with her mother's credit card because she did not want her husband to know about her visit. To me, this was the biggest sign of the true problem. Clearly, if you withhold the truth from someone, you're not communicating and you don't really want to be known. When I explained this to Jane, she began to understand that the communication problem wasn't all with her husband. She started to realize that *she* was a big part of the problem— that she was the one who was making it impossible for her husband to really know *her*, not to mention her wants and needs. She assumed her husband would not "approve" of certain things she did, so she avoided speaking with him about these things. She was sabotaging their marriage by hiding. I encouraged her to speak with her husband and asked her to stop analyzing all the ways in which he did not understand her. I wanted Jane to focus instead on the ways in which he *did* show that he loved and understood her.

Her next visit proved this theory to be true, for when she told him about our time together, he insisted on having a session too! Jane had been certain that her thoughts were the reality of the situation, when in fact it was *her* fearful thoughts that created the disconnect with her husband. Jane had closed herself off from her husband, when all he wanted was to be *let in* her life. Soon she and her husband began to develop a relationship that was honest and real. The hiding had ended, and Jane began to learn to use her mind as a tool—not a weapon.

Living Outside the Box

Many times in my life I questioned my direction. I tried to analyze how to use my gifts. I began to understand that the happiest and most successful people don't live in their minds when I was studying with Elisabeth Kübler-Ross in the early eighties. The author of *On Death and Dying*, Elisabeth was in the forefront of the hospice movement. I would watch her as she would help process the extreme grief of people who lost loved ones, or sit by the bed of an eight-year-old child dying of cancer, and then come back to the hotel and teach other people how to work with the dying. Later, in her room, I would find her wonderfully at peace, knitting a scarf or hat for a dying child. Elisabeth was doing her life's work, and it flowed naturally from her without any apparent effort or thought. She lived her life following the same guidance that she offered the people she tended to: there is no time to analyze life when there is so little of it left to live. Elisabeth had endless amounts of energy because she was in her heart, not her mind, and watching her, I saw the way I wanted to live. I realized that I could not use my mind to serve and needed to learn to quiet my mind so that I could begin to really listen to my heart.

Like a lot of us, many of my clients were taught in their formative years that a certain set course of actions was required for having a "good" life, and that it was their duty to find it and fulfill it. But often the people who followed this set course did not find the happiness, peace, or joy that had been promised. They didn't listen to what their own inner voices were telling them along the way. Instead, the heart took a back seat to the mind, and the people did as they were told. Interestingly, I have found that many of the most successful people I've met have shunned these traditional steps and have written their own rules, letting their spirits lead them "outside the box."

My clients Katherine and Jessica illustrate the difference between living in the mind and living in the heart. Katherine accepted her parents' idea of the steps to the traditional "perfect life": a college education, a business career, marriage and children. Mostly to please her parents, Katherine set out to fulfill this recipe for happiness, going to work for a major corporation right after graduating from college. It wasn't too long before she found herself in an enviable position at the top of her company.

But Katherine was very fearful. She lived in her mind. She was a very logical and analytical woman who did not believe in magic. Katherine worked diligently for her company for years, often with very little vacation, romance, or fun along the way. Though she had attained her professional goals by her late thirties. Katherine thought she should be married with children, and she couldn't understand why she wasn't in a relationship. She felt attractive, but she had not had a date in years. Because Katherine was always in her mind, she noticed couples everywhere she went, which made her even more aware of her situation. She thought about it and focused on it so much that she felt very alone and disconnected, sadly realizing that her recipe for happiness was missing some of the most essential ingredients.

On the other hand, Jessica, the woman who referred Katherine to me, was the total opposite. Jessica had followed her own inner spirit. She was always taking chances and didn't allow others to define the rules or set the course for her life. Jessica lived life wherever it took her, even changing jobs several times within a five-year period. Forty and single, Jessica desired marriage as much as Katherine, but she did not view her life with "lack." Jessica's life was very full; she was always being asked out on dates, traveling, and doing new things. Jessica looked at life as an adventure, and knew that in due time she would meet the right person and marry.

When Jessica came to work in Katherine's office, Katherine initially found Jessica's approach to life very frightening, because Katherine's narrow, traditional way of looking at life would never allow her to take such chances. But through our work together, Katherine came to realize that the patterns of her life were no longer serving her. She decided to live a bit more like Jessica and made some changes, quieting her mind and tapping into her magic to hear what her inner voice was telling her. Katherine quickly realized that her job had never quite fed her spirit, and it was time for her to quit. She decided to rent a cottage in a beach community clear on the other side of the country—with no job or any advance plans! Instead of overanalyzing every step she takes, Katherine is throwing away her traditional life recipe and taking each day as it comes, writing her own rules. Katherine is creating magic as I write.

I find Katherine's and Jessica's stories interesting for so many reasons—mostly because of the amazing way they ended up at the same place, though by such different paths and experiences. One had a lot of fun along the way, while the other did not. One believed in magic and the other did not. The takeaway from their stories is that if you stay in your mind or follow dreams other than your own, you will create a patterned existence, but you will not create a life. Most of all, you will not be creating *your* life.

Worry Is Negative Prayer

Worrying about our problems can keep us stuck; worrying about other people can be harmful to others and keep them stuck. When we worry about someone, we send a negative prayer directly to that person. On a clairvoyant level, worrying looks like your head is surrounded by knots, and you send these knots to whomever you worry about. If you send a negative prayer to someone, you are affirming his or her weakness. It does not help; in fact, it has the potential of making things harder. You may think that you're sending energy, but you are pulling it away. The concern that you feel when you worry is poisonous to both you and the person you're worried about. Just think about someone you know who worries about you. How does it feel? Not very good, right?

Lydia, a fifty-six-year-old legal secretary who was suffering from chronic fatigue syndrome, told me she was worried sick about her youngest child, Jason. Although he was almost thirty, Jason was still living at home because he had a learning disability and just never seemed to be able to hold a job. Lydia thought about retiring because her health was not great and she did not like her job, but she felt that she could not stop working because she worried about how her son would get along without her there to support him. Does this sound logical to you? After working with the Seven Keys, Lydia came back to me to tell me she had decided to quit her job and move to Florida, a location that had always given her a lot of peace. Later she reported that after she moved, her son got a job and was doing very well. Her worry had been holding him back!

We all need positive thoughts directed toward us, especially when we have challenges. Wouldn't it be better to just send a life-affirming thought instead of worrying? Just try it and see what happens! Negative prayer consumes a tremendous amount of energy for both the giver and the receiver, and it gives nothing back in return. I would much rather have someone say, "Oh, I just know that you're going to do it!" or "I'm sending positive wishes your way for you to have what you want!"

One of the most amazing people I have ever known is my client Amy, who had already gone through two brain surgeries and had given birth to a little girl when she was referred to me. Amy has brain cancer, and when we first started speaking, she had spent a great deal of effort researching and analyzing her illness. While it was helpful to gain some understanding, her search for more knowledge had developed into an obsession, and Amy soon came to realize that it was limiting her life and the lives of her husband and her baby. After we started working on the Seven Keys, she had her third surgery. Through using my keys to Life Magic, she began to understand the power of her thoughts, and she made a conscious decision to let go of all the analyzing and to discourage those around her from worrying. Amy has a huge, very close Italian family, and they were worried sick; I know this because I have spoken to many of them. She decided that when anybody told her that they were worried, she would encourage them to send her positive, life-affirming thoughts. Friends and family expected her to be worried but instead were shocked to find her filled with strength and courage. She grew more peaceful as her thoughts and her mind came into harmony. This peace in the face of such a malignant form of cancer is amazing. She finds joy in every day and is an inspiration to everyone whose life she touches. As her health continues to improve, not only has Amy stopped her own worrying, but her whole family has chosen to stop living in fear.

Recognizing Fear

The biggest obstacle to our sending out positive prayers is our fear. Fear is a weapon we turn on ourselves and others. Every day, I receive calls or visits from people from all over the world. I can tell you that the most common denominator in their messages is fear. Fear is global. Fear knows no financial barriers. Fear knows no age. Fear is not color-blind or saved just for "special people." It is everywhere. It permeates into everyone's life. People, everywhere, are looking for ways to move beyond their fears.

I do not want to analyze fear, but I do want to help expose it so you can recognize it and stop giving in to it. Fear comes between you and your magic. It creates a disconnect that keeps you from knowing just how loved you are. You must learn to trust, knowing that deep down you are safe and very loved. Don't allow fear to let you think that you have made a wrong decision, for there are no wrong decisions. Don't allow fear to make you think that you have made a mistake, for there are no mistakes. You must begin to feel fear as soon as it arrives, so that you can acknowledge it and then send it on its way!

I want us to examine fear a bit closer so that you can learn how to recognize it and remove it before it can get stored in the body and do any more damage. In order to recognize fear, you must understand how it can manifest in six different forms: judgment, anxiety, indifference, indecision, perfectionism, and confusion.

Judgment: More than ever, these days we seem to want to label and critique everything and everyone—even going so far as creating television shows just to scrutinize and rate the outfits that stars wear to the Oscars! It seems that no one is really free from judgment, which makes it all the more important that we learn not to judge. I think that people believe that judging somehow makes the world an easier place to understand, but it really doesn't help anyone, for as soon as we start to judge, we begin to see ourselves as separate. Judgment ruins that natural desire within all of us to be connected. We all have the same needs and desires to be understood, accepted, and—most of all—loved. So why separate us by judging?

When a person or situation comes up that we do not understand, isn't it better to reserve judgment and remind ourselves that everyone is here together, learning? Instead of instantly making an assumption, we should try to keep an open heart and mind in order to understand what is truly going on. Our assumptions can easily determine the end of the story before we even have a chance to experience it! But so often our assumptions turn out to be wrong, and I can say this from personal experience. I remember attending a party many years ago with a man I was dating at the time. Many of my clients were at this party too. My date and I spoke when we first arrived, but for the rest of the evening, he talked to everyone but me. If he hadn't occasionally given me a smile and nod from across the way, I would have thought I had come to the party by myself! At the end of the evening, I told him how abandoned I felt. He looked at me very surprised and said, "I can understand how you are feeling, but that is not at all where I was coming from. I certainly didn't mean to ignore you. I just wanted to give you time to be with your friends and clients. I was supporting you and your work."

It was so thoughtful, really. He didn't mean to ignore me or hurt my feelings. But even greater than that, he was showing that he cared about me far more than I had given him credit for. He was giving me freedom and support. I chose to see and feel the separation of his actions, which was an illusion anyway. My mind did what the mind so naturally does: it sought separation and a reason to close my heart. I would have been able to see this love had I not judged his actions. Again, this is further evidence that whatever we think is what we will see.

Anxiety: Anxiety is one of the more difficult versions of fear to calm down. When fear gets stored in the body, it causes us to freeze up or close down. Fear is so unnatural that it quickly short-circuits our nervous system, sending ripples of energy in a chaotic, sporadic way. When this charged up fear is left unattended or un-acknowledged, it can cause debilitating anxiety and panic attacks, usually after we project into the future or look back into the past.

Many clients come to me experiencing attacks of anxiety. They are beside themselves with fear in the form of worry, impatient and full of questions. In order to stop the projections into the past and future, we work hard on stabilizing the mind to stay in the present moment. I tell them to grip the arms of their chair and imagine they can breathe into their feet. Becca came to me after her first anxiety attack left her worried she was going to have another. Becca spent a great deal of time worrying about money, but she was giving the universe mixed messages about money with her thoughts. In Becca's unconscious, money equaled fear. So on one hand she was saying she wanted money, while on the other she was thinking that the subject of money made her afraid.

After I asked Becca to focus on and analyze the times she did not feel anxiety, her attacks stopped. I also gave her this easy way to recognize fear when it comes into the body, before it can turn into anxiety.

Exercise Your Spirit:	The Prick of the Thorn
What you will need:	You
Time:	5 minutes

- *Close your eyes and think of a beautiful rose.*
- *Admire its beauty and breathe in its rich fragrance.*
- *Notice how open and free you feel as you observe the beauty of the rose.*
- *Now, think of the rose's thorn.*
- *Imagine that its sharp point pricks you.*
- *Notice how your body closes or freezes up. This is the feeling that you must recognize. This is how fear starts to enter your body.*
- *Go back to the rose and open it back up and breathe. Notice how you can open your body back up with your thoughts.*

Indifference: After fear sets in, it can move into indifference, which basically means you have a lack of interest or concern. It may feel safe to not care anymore. For instance, your mind often does not believe that you deserve to have love. You may tell yourself that you "don't want to get your hopes up." Consider the example of my client Gwen, a Hollywood producer. Gwen has wanted to meet her life partner for some time now, yet was growing more and more frustrated because she hadn't met "him" yet. Finally, she said to me, "Laura, maybe I am just meant to be alone. Maybe this is my path and I just need to learn to accept it." Gwen was postponing her good. She was becoming indifferent to her own desire. I said, "Gwen, don't say that! You must believe in your good! Go buy a robe for 'him' and hang it in your closet. And while you are at it, make sure that you have some pretty underwear and a nice gown too. Start acting as if you already have this man in your life. Concentrate not on the lack but on creating your future."

She took my advice, and within six weeks she had started dating several interesting men. Before this, she hadn't had a single date in over a year. Her indifference was sending mixed messages to the universe. But once the message was clarified, the universe responded, and at last report she was seeing someone very seriously.

Indecision: When fear manifests itself within us as indecision, the mind sees so many options that it cannot just sit still and listen to the heart. For example, my client Tommy would come in to talk to me about his career. Tommy was not sure what he should do. He was trying to decide whether he should go back to law school or continue teaching junior high. While Tommy was content in his current job, it wasn't his passion. Tommy loves anything to do with law and genuinely lights up when he speaks about it. He had actually discovered his passion, but the questions plagued him. He wondered, "How will I find the money needed to pay the hefty law school tuition?" "How about the fact that there are already so many lawyers?" "What am I thinking, giving up my secure teaching position for such an unknown?" "What if I cannot pass the LSAT?" "What if I am wrong and I'm not happy practicing law?"

The questions and indecision were enough to give Tommy a headache! I asked Tommy, "How are you ever going to know unless you do it?" He needed to leave the indecision behind and move on to make a decision—any type of decision. Decisions are not set in concrete. It is always OK for us to make another decision if we are not at peace with the first one. Otherwise, indecision will always hold us back: fear will hold us back.

Thank goodness that Tommy listened to his heart. He is currently in law school, enjoying the study of law and having positive thoughts about his future.

Perfectionism: While at first blush it may not seem like fear, perfectionism is a form of fear used by many to try to control life. Insisting on perfection keeps us from getting very far. Plus it encourages us to indulge in judgment in its grandest form—self-judgment. Remember this: love is perfect, so you do not have to be!

My client Jim is the owner of a very profitable company. Well educated, well traveled, and well known, he dresses impeccably and drives a Mercedes-Benz. He exemplifies what many would consider to be the "perfect life." Yet if you ask Jim, he would not say he is successful; he is a perfectionist, forever nitpicking at his life. Instead of enjoying the success of his company, Jim complains about his employees, whom he uniformly regards as difficult, incompetent, and unqualified to participate in the decision-making process. Then he complains about having to make all the decisions on his own!

Jim's perfectionism extends into his personal life as well. We all know someone like Jim, so it probably won't surprise you to learn that he has twice broken off engagements after finding fault with the women with whom he had once fallen in love. Jim spends most of his time looking at all that is wrong with his life. Jim would be far better off living his life with lower expectations and coming to understand that we all are OK with our little imperfections. After all, nobody is perfect.

Jim, who is currently working with the Seven Keys, has moved back into a relationship he ended several years before our introduction. He realized he had given someone up whom he still loved. I gave him a technique that I have used successfully through the years; it draws on the power of the rose (a very romantic flower). I consider the fragrance of the rose to be the highest vibration on the planet. It is wonderful for squelching fears or eliminating negative thoughts. Many of my clients have found that whenever they smell it, they instantly feel better (unless, of course, they have had some negative association or allergy to roses). I'd like you to try this simple way of quickly removing fear.

Exercise Your Spirit:	**Rose Water**
What you will need:	**Rose water with a sprayer**
Time:	**Ongoing**

- *Whenever you find yourself in fear, whether it is worrying, judging, or critiquing, spray rose water around the top of your head.*
- *After you spray the rose water, really breathe in the fragrance.*
- *Replace any negative thoughts with positive, affirming thoughts, enveloping yourself in hope, love, and encouragement.*

This act of spraying rose water really does work to erase the negativity and fear that the mind creates. It cleans off the body's energy field; more importantly, it distracts you from your negative thoughts. It stops you in your tracks, so you can't continue in this fearful thought pattern. I make sure to carry a small bottle of rose water with me at all times!

Confusion: Finally, let's look at confusion, the last form of fear we'll discuss. My client Terri is confused about everything in her life. For years she has been dating a man who cannot make a commitment. Although he moved in with her, he also chose to keep his own apartment, isn't ready to get married, and doesn't want to discuss their future. Terri's career is stuck as well. Her boss recently informed her that she would never be promoted. Terri realizes that she has gone as far as she can in the company, but she does not know what to do—at all! She is deeply confused. Should she wait for her boyfriend to commit, or should she end it? Will she ever meet anyone she feels the same about? Will she be able to find another job? If she breaks up with her boyfriend, will she be able to pay her rent without him? Terri's mind is scrambled and her whole life reflects her state of confusion. How can she receive any of the answers when she keeps putting more and more questions in the mix? Terri is a very intelligent woman, but her confusion is impeding her progress and limiting what she can receive.

Fear is keeping all of these people stuck. It is keeping them from their magic, their destiny, and their love. The good news is that fear can be removed. And once you rid your mind of the things that plague it—all these forms of fear—then you can invite the magic back in. It's like taking Windex to all the unproductive, negative words you have written on your mirror in that thick, red lipstick and washing them all away! You will then have a new beginning and can write happy and healthy messages that will bring about the life you want.

Here is a simple exercise I give my clients to help them begin to remove their fear:

Exercise Your Spirit:	Breathe Love
What you will need:	You
Time:	15 minutes

- *As you exhale, breathe out fear.*
- *When you inhale, bring in love.*
- *See the love as a soft pink energy and visualize the fear as a thick gray energy.*
- *Breathe out the gray that is in your body until it is all gone—always replacing it with the soft pink love.*

Use Your Imagination

When you saw the energies of love and fear in shades of pink and gray in the above exercise, you took an important step in your magic, the step of using your imagination to help you heal and grow. Do you remember having a vivid imagination as a child? Do you feel as if you have lost your sense of imagination somewhere along the way? Imagination is a very important part of magic, but it is usually dismissed or discounted as we become adults. You may have grown up hearing, "Don't be silly! That is just your imagination." I am surprised by how little people use their imagination. I remember telling a young female client, "I can see someone sending you flowers," only to hear her respond, "Ah, flowers—I can't even imagine someone sending me flowers." Imagine—not being able to imagine receiving flowers! It is no wonder she never received them.

It is interesting that when I ask clients to use their imagination, sometimes they reject it, saying, "This is useless," or "I want something real, not imaginary." They do not realize that imagination *is* a reality; it *is* a capacity; and it *is* a potentiality within everyone. You really *can* imagine. Imagination is a very powerful tool to help you find your magic. It's there for you to harness and use to your good.

Through your imagination you can either sabotage your life or you can create *magic* in your life! It all depends on you. Remember, you are broadcasting a signal sent out from within that returns to you, the sender. Most people spend a great deal more time looking at and listening to how others manifest their dreams—via music, books, business success stories, sports, television and movies—than they do using their imagination to bring their own desires into being. You literally pay others for dreaming. If you spent just half as much time using your imagination, you would be living the life of your dreams!

Often people don't understand what imagination really is. Imagination is just a very intense focus that brings together your intuitive and mental qualities with the desires of your heart. It is not the same as fantasy. Fantasizing is pretending that something is happening that you know could never ever happen. A young client came in feeling that she was going to marry the actor Hugh Grant.

That is fantasy. Now, if she used her imagination, she could begin to see herself with someone who had some of the same characteristics as Hugh Grant. That would be imagination! Imagination enables you to act as if something were actually true. In other words, imagination is getting into an attitude so completely that the attitude becomes your reality.

I created an imagination exercise to help me in an area that I felt weak in. For many years, I did not feel sexy. Because I was working and traveling all the time, I was not going on any dates. Nor did I feel that I was being noticed as a woman. And believe me, my life reflected my beliefs about myself! So one day I had an idea: why not try to imagine myself as someone whom I considered sexy? I decided to embody the same characteristics that someone sexy would have and to feel what someone sexy would feel inside. Instantly, Sophia Loren seemed like the perfect person to imagine. So I pictured Sophia Loren on my left, the side of the body that is the feminine or receptive side. I began imagining that I could breathe her essence into my body. I imagined that I had that sexy warmth that Sophia so naturally exudes. I did this for a few minutes, two times a day. After nearly six weeks of this exercise, I attended a wedding in San Francisco. At the rehearsal dinner, a man at the microphone pointed to me and said, "I would like that sexy woman in the blue dress to make a toast." I was floored. Not only was I being singled out in a room full of beautiful people, but also he had labeled me with the exact image I had been going for: sexy. It worked! Now I am married to a man who feels that I am the sexiest woman alive, but—more importantly—I feel sexy! I have shared this little exercise with many of my clients, who used it with great success. I invite you to try it too.

Exercise Your Spirit:	Someone You Admire
What you will need:	You
Time:	A few minutes a day, two times a day for two weeks.

- *Close your eyes and think of someone in your field of work whom you admire or someone who has a trait that you wish to empower in yourself.*
- *Imagine the characteristics that that person exudes every day, the characteristics that create that trait.*
- *Picture that person on the left side of your body.*
- *In your mind's eye, hold the image of that person and breathe him or her into your body.*
- *Allow yourself to feel the energy of the person.*
- *For the next two weeks, at least two times a day, do this simple exercise. You will soon find yourself opening up that energy or trait within yourself.*

Warning: this exercise is very powerful! Imagination is an energy and a force that your mind moves through. Once the mind links with the imagination, the body will follow, and your dreams will soon become reality.

Quieting Your Mind

Before we can really create our magic, we must train the mind to get out of our way—to stop sending prayers that we don't really want to be answered, and to stop thinking negative thoughts that limit us. We do this by quieting the mind. Your thinking has to be turned off for your spirit to be heard. Once your mind is emptied of all its negative thoughts, you can rediscover and claim your magic. We do this with two practices: breathing and meditation.

Do you realize how much a part of the universe you are? We are all deeply connected by our breath. We all live in the same ocean of air. All that we are reverberates throughout and we all share in each other—all the darkness and negativity, and all the light and joy. We actually breathe each and every one of these things into our heart. It's the world's heart, after all. This is a method of magic that utilizes alchemy to heal: breathing in the entire world's suffering and then transmuting it with the compassion of our heart.

Exercise Your Spirit:	**Benediction**
What you will need:	**You**
Time:	**10 minutes**

- *I want you to relax into your entire being because you are being cherished by the whole universe.*
- *Take in a big, deep, full breath and breathe in all the suffering of the world.*
- *When you exhale your breath, I want you to breathe out all the joy, all the peace, and all the benediction that you have within you.*
- *Breathe out and pour yourself into the universe's existence.*

You will make a surprising discovery when you do this exercise: the moment you inhale, you are able to tap into your own healing energy and turn the suffering you breathed in into joy. If you're already familiar with breathing and meditation, you probably remember being told to breathe in love and breathe out pain. As powerful an experience that can be, you don't have to breathe in love all the time. We all have the power to transform pain into love; the heart is a calming force, and it immediately transforms the energy. We should all drink in the misery and transform it into blessings that we can then pour out into the world. You will realize how much the universe loves you and needs your love in return.

This is why your magical spirit goes on breathing and pulsating within you. Once you start feeling this tremendous connection with the world, you will start feeling safe. You will discover your inner magic and you will trust yourself. You will become enlightened—magical! Enlightenment is not something you have to work for, for if you relax for even a moment, you will find that you are already enlightened. It is just your nature. Enlightenment cannot be planned for: it is already there, patiently waiting for you!

If you can allow yourself to breathe into every aspect that represents the fullness of your life—the depth, wonder, beauty, craziness, and strife—you can live fearlessly. You will come to realize that if you just keep breathing, you cannot be conquered. You can actually breathe your way through life!

Many of us don't realize that we are not breathing fully and have no idea how this lack is affecting the rest of our life. Lisa was a recently divorced, forty-six-year-old corporate lawyer when she first came to me. She had already spent a lot of time analyzing and thinking about her life, having gone to therapy twice a week for the past ten years. After working with Lisa for a while, I came to understand what was keeping her stuck. She was in her head, thinking far too much!

Lisa was living in her mind, not her heart, and the noise of her mind was getting in her way. I compared her problem to that of a computer: every day, Lisa was busy searching and indexing her hard drive. She knew every file in that drive backward and forward. She knew what issues from her past were affecting her present life. She was certain she knew the reason for everything. Lisa was so busy using the files that had been stored in her computer for the past forty-six years that she was not downloading any new files or updates. Nor was Lisa erasing any of the old programs. In fact, she was using the same old programs every day.

I'm not saying that therapy isn't valuable. Lisa was actually referred to me by her therapist, who felt that her training didn't prepare her to move Lisa to the next stage. I am certain that Lisa would not have been ready for me without the therapy. She would not have been able to let go of her mind—and all those files!

Breathe Well to Live Well

In working with Lisa, I noticed that her breathing was very shallow. We should all look after our breathing, because it is one of the most important things that we, as humans, do. It sustains our life. If you are not breathing fully, you are not living fully: you're holding something back from life and not fully receiving life in return. And since we breathe when we communicate, how can we communicate fully if we're not breathing fully? Once again, if we don't communicate fully, something will be held back of what we give and receive.

Lisa wanted to move into her body and stop the shallow breathing, so she began using the following exercise to allow her breath—and in turn, her life—to become more peaceful and rich.

Exercise Your Spirit:	**Breathe Them Away**
What you will need:	**You**
Time:	**Ongoing**

This exercise helps you practice breathing away all thoughts.

- *Close your eyes.*
- *No doubt a thousand and one thoughts will come across the canvas of your mind.*
- *Let all these thoughts pass you by without giving them any energy or attention—like watching a train passing by.*
- *When your mind is quiet and your body is still, exhale completely.*
- *Hold your lungs empty until you feel as if you will burst. (It is not harmful to hold your breath if you do so consciously.)*
- *Inhale deeply and fully to the tips of your toes.*
- *Repeat this exercise seven more times.*

Three months of weekly meetings with Lisa brought about profound results. She became softer and more feminine. She began to smile and give hugs to everyone in my office! Lisa started following her heart. People still come to see me who witnessed firsthand the dramatic changes that Lisa made so quickly. It all started when Lisa corrected her breathing, which allowed her to quiet her mind and move into her heart.

Many people do not breathe deeply; instead of using their diaphragm, they use shallow or chest breathing, which minimizes their intake of oxygen and causes stress and anxiety as a result. *Diaphragmatic* or *abdominal* breathing is a way of using our bodies as nature intended: the diaphragm moves down on the in-breath, expanding the space in the chest so that more air can fill the lungs. On the out-breath, the diaphragm moves upward, pushing the air out of the lungs. To achieve this, concentrate primarily on the out-breath, which should be calm, long, and deep; during the exhalation, feel yourself exert a free, relaxed, expanding downward pressure on the lower internal organs, without pulling in the abdomen. The in-breath should be natural and spontaneous: the lungs will quickly fill with air again, because they are mostly empty.

Air contains the energy of the universal life force that is received by every cell of our bodies, so it's very important to develop our breathing. The main objective in controlling your breath is to establish balance, so that the inflow and outflow become even. Focusing on your breathing also helps you regulate and slow down your mind when it is racing. It's a good thing to do before you come home from a busy day, to clear your head so you can be *with* the people you love instead of just being next to them.

Bringing in the breath also starts subtly to bring you into your body. When you're in your mind all the time, you are not really in the body. But when you start to focus your breathing, you begin to receive life, to breathe into your soul, which holds all the magic, all the secrets of your destiny. Breathing is really about bringing your life to you. You don't think about doing it, but you're bringing yourself closer to your destiny.

The Magic of Meditation

Breathing also prepares us for meditation, a link between mind and spirit that you can train your mind to make. When you achieve this connection, your mind will settle down into quietness, and you will gradually and effortlessly discover your spirit. This calming of the mind will bring corresponding benefits to your body. When you breathe freely and quiet your mind, you can actually change your thought patterns. Meditation is the time we listen for answers, just as prayer is the time we ask for them. But we can't always be asking, asking, asking without ever listening, or we'll never hear what the universe has to say to us.

Many people have said to me that they don't know how to meditate properly—that they can't "get there" or they end up falling asleep. I can appreciate this reaction because meditation is not necessarily easy. Nothing has changed my own life as much as when I finally learned to quiet my mind. I will never forget the day, after months of practice, that my mind finally silenced itself in meditation. When my mind became completely still, my spirit was allowed to engage fully. I experienced my inner flame for the first time and truly understood who I was. It was a beautiful moment. I pray that all of you will have this same experience.

Meditation has two parts. The first part is like cleaning a house. You must take an inventory of what you have. It is often a good idea to make a list of your positive and negative traits. Our first task is to know ourselves. Without self-knowledge there can be no development on a higher level. In the next exercise, you will look at the positive and negative sides of yourself. You will create two psychological mirrors reflecting these two sides, which are for you and you alone to see. The recognition of these two sides to your personality is absolutely necessary if you are to attain the magic equipoise, and the further development of magical skills depends on it.

Exercise Your Spirit:	An Exercise of Introspection
What you will need:	Your Magic Notebook
Time:	2 weeks

- *In your magic notebook, write down all the bad sides of your personality. This diary should be kept private. It is for your own use only and must not be shown to anybody else. In looking at your failures, habits, passions, instincts, and any character traits you find offensive in yourself, you have to adopt a hard and honest attitude toward yourself.* Do not embellish any of your failures and deficiencies.
- *In quiet meditation, put yourself back into different situations of your past, remembering how you behaved and what mistakes you might have made.*
- *Make notes of all your weaknesses, down to the finest nuances and variations. Nothing must remain hidden, however insignificant or great your faults or frailties may be. The more you discover, the better for you.*

- *Spray yourself with rose water after you write each day. At the end of one week you will have a list of offenses. We will use this list in Key Four when we talk about the fire element.*
- *During the next week, repeat the same procedure with your good qualities, entering them into the magic notebook.*
- *At the end of one week, you will have a list of positive qualities. Focus on these positive qualities from this point forth.*

You must make room in your mind for all the positive thoughts you want to keep, because with no filter, all thoughts will continue going through your mind. Keep only the thoughts you want and remove the others. Clean your mind as if you are cleaning your whole house. Purify it with silence. After you have "cleaned out the house," then await the magic. Then, surprise! You will find that the magic is already there. It has been there all the time—just waiting for enough room to get your attention!

These next exercises will further prepare you for meditation. Take your time with them, so that you learn to meditate and breathe properly. Meditation happens when your mind quiets.

Exercise Your Spirit:	**Clear Your Mind**
What you will need:	**A quiet place, free of distraction**
Time:	**Ongoing**

Follow these three steps, making sure to complete each step before proceeding to the next.

Step 1

- *This step teaches you to not give in to unwanted thoughts. For instance, you must not allow yourself to think about work when you leave to go home at night or on the weekend.*
- *All thoughts not belonging to your private life must be set aside so that you will begin to allow yourself to relax. When you find your mind wandering back, just breathe the thought out of your mind.*
- *And just the other way around, in your job, all your thoughts should be concentrated on work. You must not allow your thoughts to digress or wander back to home or private affairs. When an unwanted thought starts to come back, breathe it away.*
- *Practice this exercise each day for seven minutes, and then keep extending it.*
- *This exercise should be kept for a lifetime, because it sharpens the mind and strengthens your consciousness and memory.*

Step 2

- *After you have practiced step one, you can expand to think a single thought or idea for a length of time. Some examples:* I am at peace, or I am learning to love myself totally . . .
- *Don't let any other thoughts come into your mind.*

- *You can choose any train of thought or idea for this exercise.*
- *Hold on to the thought that you chose with all your strength.*
- *Refuse all other thoughts.*
- *At first you will probably only be able to hold the thought for a few seconds, but later on, you will find you can hold it for minutes.*
- *Your goal is to concentrate on one single thought and follow it for 10 minutes. This exercise, with practice, will help you to enhance your clarity and concentration.*

Step 3

- *The last step in clearing your mind is to learn how to produce an absolute vacancy of mind. The path is very simple: get out of your mind as many times a day and as often as possible.*
- *Lie down comfortably on a bed or sit in an armchair and relax your whole body.*
- *Close your eyes.*
- *Dismiss any thought coming upon you. If you watch a thought, it arises one moment and the next moment it is gone. Let it go.*
- *Nothing at all is allowed to happen in your mind; there must be absolute vacancy.*
- *Now hold on to this stage of vacancy.*
- *At first you will manage to do so for a few seconds only.*

- *The purpose of this exercise, which is to begin to listen to your spirit, will be attained when you succeed in remaining in this state for a full ten minutes without losing your self-control or falling asleep.*

If you want to become acquainted with yourself, you must learn the simple art of being silent. The moment you are perfectly silent, your life goes through a radical change. In the beginning, the silence may feel like sadness. You have been so used to being active, engaged, and busy that when all this activity dies down, you may feel as if you have lost everything. Clearing your mind is like a surgery—taking out the stored pain to bring you back in touch with your magic.

Be just a little bit patient and allow this sadness to settle. This process is actually the beginning of silence, the beginning of meditation. As the sadness settles, you will start enjoying the peace. The sadness is just the emptying of the ego, and it will begin to turn to peace as you clear away the noise of your mind. You will begin to feel good about yourself. Remember, we do not receive things in order to feel good. We have to *feel* good so we can receive things. As your mind quiets and you move into your heart, you will feel more innocent—more childlike.

As a child, I used to spend countless hours looking up at the clouds. Today, even as an adult, I still look up in the sky every day and see signs and symbols. Know that we aren't searching for paradise in the clouds; rather, we must bring the magic of the clouds down to Earth and make a paradise here. Please mark this page, because in the next chapter, we will refer to this exercise as we create your magic and move into your heart.

Exercise Your Spirit:	**Clouds**
What you will need:	**Your magic notebook**
Time:	**However long**
	you want!

- *Look up in the clouds today and see if you can discern an animal or a symbol.*
- *Find your animal or symbol in the sky.*
- *Write down the exact day that you looked up to the sky and what animal or symbol you saw. Write about what you saw in great detail. Even sketch it out if you want!*
- *Then write down what you were thinking about when you saw it.*

When you quiet your mind, you naturally begin to listen to your heart. The next key will help you understand your heart and connect to the light—the love—that burns within you.

CHAPTER 3

KEY 3: Your Heart Is Your Lantern

Let your light shine. Shine within so that you can shine on someone else. Let your light shine.

—OPRAH WINFREY

The time has come to listen to your heart. Your heart provides you with the insight and power to move toward your true life, to find your way into a magical world. When you're listening to your heart, you are feeling your life, not analyzing it. With practice, this can be as simple as just checking in with yourself once in a while and asking, *How do I feel right now?* Your inner voice gets stronger as you keep listening and clearing away the noise inside your head from all the emotions you've accumulated through your life. When you connect with your heart, you will know what is true and right for you. Your magic is a deep desire that will just keep following you around until you listen. You have been waiting for yourself all these years!

Understanding your heart will lead you into working with the light of the universe. When you are connected to the light, your dreams become a reality. But even greater than that, you will be connected to everyone else who embraces the light. You will not be alone: you will be a soul that understands, heals, and uplifts others. I can tell you this with absolute certainty, because I have been watching the energy field of the human body my whole life. We are all connected: I can see it!

Think of your heart as your battery—the source of the electrical force that puts the spark of life into us all. Your heart keeps you alive, nurturing and sustaining you with energy and warmth so that you can follow your soul path. Just behind your physical heart is your spiritual heart, which connects you to your soul. When your spiritual heart is open, it sparkles with a warm golden glow. The more you quiet your mind and open your heart, the more your spiritual center fills with this luminous life force. It burns within you like a lantern, providing light for your journey, shining like a beacon for others to see.

You've probably noticed this light in other people. We've all met people who exude a natural warmth, whose inner beauty immediately shines through. Their energy has an almost magnetic force that feels good to be around. Those are people whose hearts are full, their lights burning bright. Now is the time to cultivate your own luminescence. The fuller and more open your heart is, the brighter it can shine for you and for others to follow.

Some call this light "God," some call it "Allah," some call it "Buddha," and some call it "Jesus." No matter what your belief, all these names for the light of the heart share the same meaning, for they all represent a force of love. Learning to love is the reason we're all created, so when we are disconnected from this force of love, we can feel separated from our purpose, lost in a world of fear. When you are connected to this love or light, however, you can move through anything—yes, *anything*—with grace.

When you follow your heart, your life flows like water, the element that represents the feelings of your heart. To show you how important this element is, consider that almost 80 percent of your body is made up of water. You are literally a body of water. Consider our planet as well: 70 percent of the earth is covered in water. And just as every river must move to the ocean, your life must flow toward your destiny. Your life is either a river or a pond. If you have become a pond, closed to the flow of life, you may have forgotten your destiny. You may have forgotten how to listen.

Chinese astrologers say that water is the most powerful element because it is perfectly nonresistant: when it is surging, water can sweep up everything in its way; over time, water can wear away the most solid rock. A heart full of love is just as strong. Water can teach you how to flow if you ask it. It is the element of cleansing, healing, and love. Water gives us life when we are thirsty; its energy is vital to our well-being. Still, many of us do not give ourselves the water that our bodies need. This simple exercise can help you learn to appreciate the essential role of water—of flow—in your life. Join me in asking water to be part of our journey.

Exercise Your Spirit:	**Water Blessing**
What you will need:	**A bowl**
Time:	**10–15 minutes**

- *Fill a bowl with water and place it before you as you sit in a comfortable position.*
- *Put your finger in the water and taste it.*

- *Put your hand in the water. Feel its temperature and its softness.*
- *Take a handful and release it back into the bowl. As you listen to the calming sound of the water, remember that we are made of water.*
- *Say this chant out loud:*
  Dear Element of water:

> *Play and bubble in my heart*
> *Teach me that not one of us lives apart*
>
> *Bring me back into the flow*
> *Life goes on—I have to know*
>
> *Oh, great moon I see above*
> *Teach me how to really love*
>
> *Please, sweet water, play and cleanse*
> *My heart to grow, my soul to mend.*

- *As you work with this key, notice your intake of water. Increase it and be aware of how much better you feel. Take baths and showers with appreciation as water cleanses and purifies you.*

The more comfortable you feel with the fluid part of your life, the more ease you'll have feeling the love in your heart. Jasmine came to me as a twenty-four-year-old student who was deathly afraid of water. Her father had thrown her into a swimming pool when she was about three years old, and because of her fear she had avoided swimming lessons and many summer activities. As you can imagine, Jasmine also had difficulty trusting men—so much so that she had never had a relationship. As she began to call the water element into her life, she decided to learn to swim. After six months at the local YWCA she became a regular swimmer. This release of fear opened her eyes to many new things, and shortly after she began swimming, she had her first date in three years!

You don't have to become a swimmer to be restored by water's healing energies. When Amanda first came to see me, her whole life revolved around work. A busy, overweight divorce lawyer, she rarely saw the light of day from anywhere but her office window. At the age of forty-eight, she was lost in almost every aspect of her life except her career. More than that, Amanda had lost contact with the elements: the earth, the air, water, and fire. After working with the Seven Keys, she got in touch with the elements, and began to use them as a way of finding her inner child and having fun again. It had been so long! Amanda made many changes in her life, sold her home, and moved closer to the water, so she could walk on the beach in the mornings before work. She looks about ten years younger and is thirty pounds lighter than when she first walked into my office months ago. Amanda has found her balance and has discovered that by working less, she is actually making more money than ever. But no amount of money could compare to her newfound joy! Amanda needed to reconnect to the water element and to what she really loved so that her life was not just about work.

Courage to Change

Following your heart can take courage, because it may require you to make some life changes. If you have been asking for change, get ready! Sometimes what you hear your heart saying may not make sense right away. Your heart isn't logical—but this is why it can bring you to greater joy. Remember, your mind doesn't have the capacity to be happy, so don't look to logic to bring you happiness.

Mythology expert Joseph Campbell, author of *The Hero with a Thousand Faces*, said, "We must be willing to get rid of the life we planned so as to have the life that is waiting for us." I can tell you this from experience. Let me share with you how the life I planned was drastically changed. I was in my twenties when I was hospitalized with a high fever and pneumonia, unable to breathe without being connected to oxygen. One morning I awoke from a deep sleep and felt a cool breeze on my face. My body was very cold. When I reached down to pull up my blankets, I saw the Virgin Mary standing by my bed. A shrill, high-pitched hum rang in my ears. There was a bright light, but it didn't hurt my eyes; instead, it seemed somehow to open them. My heart started to burn with the same tingling sensation I experienced as a child when I had my first apparition of the Virgin. This sensation is called the Sacre Coeur or Sacred Heart, and I continue to feel it whenever she appears. It is a signal to me that I am in my magic.

This particular apparition changed my life and led me to my destiny. When the Virgin touched me, chills went up and down my spine. My eyes were wide open, so I knew it was not a dream. I remember thinking that surely a nurse would come in to check on me, but no one entered the room. I felt a wave of electricity come into my body, as my heart continued to burn. My mind tried to question all that was happening, and I looked around the room for an open window to explain my feeling so cold. My brain did this instinctually, because our minds always try to make sense of things that only our spirits can understand. But there was no open window, and finally I just let go and gave in to what I was seeing and feeling.

"You must leave your life and go do my work," the Mother said to me. *How can she ask me to do this?* I thought to myself. As soon as she said this, I saw a picture of President John F. Kennedy in my mind. Now that scared me: that didn't make any sense at all! As the Virgin continued speaking, the words *earth heart . . . earth heart . . . earth heart . . .* repeated over and over like the beat of a drum. Soon I was out of the trance, looking at the empty place beside my bed. The Virgin was gone and all I was left with was the scent of roses and my burning heart. The nurse finally came in and commented on the lovely smell of roses. I remember smelling that lush rose fragrance on my skin for days afterward.

Six months later I was hiking in Idaho when a couple on the trail struck up a conversation with me. I learned that the husband was the head of the Transpersonal Psychology Department at John F. Kennedy University, a Northern California school I had never heard of. Upon hearing the name of the school, my mind went back to my apparition. As soon as I remembered and re-called the Virgin's message of needing to leave my life, I wanted to swat this awareness away. I chose to ignore the message and con-tinued on with my traditional life.

Soon thereafter, I was at a Shakespeare Festival in Oregon, where I was seated beside a woman who not only lived right next to John F. Kennedy University but also had an empty apartment in her home. Again, my mind went back to the apparition and the pieces of the puzzle began to fill in. The seat on the other side of us remained empty until the intermission, when a nice man our age sat down and joined our conversation. He was a medical doc-tor from San Francisco—a pioneer in alternative healing. There was an unspoken comfort among the three of us, as if we had already known each other for years. On a hunch I suggested that we all have dinner together. By the end of the meal, I knew that my hunch had been more than right: my destiny had spoken.

I realized after this "coincidental" evening that I had to pay attention to my apparition and follow the prolific signs that were being shown to me. I applied to John F. Kennedy University, rented that vacant apartment, and arranged to work with the Shakespeare-loving doctor. This was a huge decision for me—the sort I never dreamed I would be making. It was incredibly difficult for me to leave my life of comfort and luxury to go live in a small apartment with a very uncertain future. But I did so, heeding the Virgin Mary's advice. The only reason I could allow myself to do this was that I trusted in her love and wisdom so completely.

For the next five years I simply traveled wherever Spirit called, following the requests for my healing from city to city. It was during this time that I was granted the opportunity to meet Mother Teresa and spend time watching a living saint in action. While I had been going to school part-time, it soon became clear to me that I had not left Idaho to go to school. Instead, the decision was meant to uproot me and put me on my path, to do the work I was meant to do.

Even though I was answering the call and strengthening my mind and abilities, this change wasn't at all easy for me. My heart ached because I was lonely beyond belief. Through the experience of being away from my family for weeks at a time, I came to learn all the more that love is a powerful force that will travel over any distance. It was a compelling lesson in unconditional love. While this part of my life was very painful, I would do it all again, if asked. I knew that I had to follow my spirit and calling, whatever the price. As do you.

Learning to Trust

Trust is the foundation of a spiritual life, and without it one cannot really have peace, joy, or gratitude. Without trust you cannot have love. Love and trust go hand in hand, like soul mates; you really can't have one without the other. Trust creates a relationship with yourself and with the universe that enables you to listen to your heart and know that what you're hearing (or thinking, or saying) is true and good for you. Then you can begin to trust that everything that happens in your life is for your good—and start to see the good in everything that happens.

Brenda Preece came to me because she was having prophetic dreams. Some of her dreams were actually predicting the future. She couldn't believe it! She wanted to know if she was psychic, but she was afraid of her newfound gifts, full of fear of what might happen if she had a "bad" dream one day. Brenda didn't know how to use her natural intuition, but when she began to trust her instincts, she learned not only to further develop her talents, but also to love and honor herself. Brenda soon became the divine healer that she was meant to be, and she set up a private practice in Sterling, Kansas, to share her gifts with others.

Trust isn't an attitude that can be passed on; you have to learn it through stepping into the unknown and finding your feet again. There are times when you are not going to feel entirely comfortable, because when we're learning how to trust we put ourselves through a lot of different experiences. This can feel like we're being tested by the universe. You've probably heard people say that they are being tested. Whenever I hear that, I think, *Who's testing whom? Do you really think there's someone up there testing you?* What's more likely is that we are testing ourselves. We are here to learn to love, thus we are here to also learn to trust.

Where hope can often serve as a ray of light, a beacon to illuminate our way through the darkness, trust is what develops as our hope repeatedly sees us through. It makes life so much easier to know that there's a perfect plan for you, to believe that everything happens in your life to help you learn to love and accept yourself as perfect. Remember, every morning you step out of bed onto a planet that's moving and spinning at an unimaginably fast speed, yet you don't even think twice about it. When you start living your life with that same kind of trust, you'll find miraculous things are happening to you all the time. You'll see that you have been surrounded by magic all your life.

My client Angie gave up the security of a very desirable job in the entertainment industry to follow her heart. As the assistant to the head of a major studio, she had the type of job that lots of people are dying to get. At the age of twenty-seven, Angie felt trapped—living on credit cards to pay off her student loans, working night and day with no time for dates or friendships, and putting up with a boss who mistreated her. In her desire to please her employer, she had allowed him to beat her down, and her self-esteem was suffering.

A very intelligent young woman with a photographic memory, Angie really wanted to go to graduate school but was afraid to let go of the prestige and security her job provided her. But once she started to trust, her life very quickly turned around. As soon as she made the decision to follow her heart, everything she needed fell into place: a place to live, a part-time job, and money to live on. One thing I have noticed is that when you follow your heart and do your life's true work, you will receive everything you need. From the magical moment Angie decided to do something she really loved, everything just fell into her lap. It took guts to follow her heart, but she has found her magic as a result. No longer carrying around the burden of her unhappiness, she looks calm, relaxed, and comfortable in her own skin; she has begun dating again, and is making straight As in school. It was as if she were sitting on a treasure trove of abundance that she couldn't see until her heart showed it to her. Now she is flowing with her life.

We Are All Learning to Love

I will never forget the day that a reporter asked Mother Teresa if there was anything that she needed to learn. I remember how surprised I was by her answer: she told him she was still learning to love herself. The secret is that none of us really knows how to love. We are all learning. I decided from that day forward to be a happy learner.

It can be a hard lesson to accept. Rachel came to me after she had inherited a large sum of money. At the age of fifty-three, she could do anything she wanted but didn't know what to do next. She asked me what she was supposed to do with her life, and I told her that she was here to love. She was not happy with that message. "Is that all?" she said. Like many of us, she did not feel worthy of just loving.

People give love in many different ways: by giving money, doing service, offering gifts, spending time, creating intimacy, connecting, and communicating. We receive love in different ways too. Think of receiving love the same way you receive a compliment. If someone tells you, "Oh, you look fabulous, I love that new look," how do you respond? Few are those who can simply accept it, taking it in with a "Thank you very much." More often people deflect it, bounce it right back at the person who gave it as if they are in a tennis match.

It doesn't matter how intelligent or successful you are if you don't feel loved and connected. You are here purely and simply to give and receive love. In all the years I sat and worked with the dying, never once did I hear someone say that he wished he had worked harder or had done one more deal. Instead, people wished they had spent more time with their families and loved ones.

The difficulty we have receiving love keeps us from our magic, especially when it comes to the love we have for ourselves. Like Mother Teresa, we are all still learning how to love ourselves. The exercises in this book are all about opening up your ability to give and receive love, including your love for yourself. Ask, and the universe will teach you how. If you wake up every day and say, "I want to learn to love myself totally," then the people who come into your life will be messengers and teachers who are here to help you learn. Believe me, desire does all the work.

Exercise Your Spirit:	**Receiving Love**
What you will need:	**A mirror**
Time:	**Ongoing**

- *Stand before the mirror and look at your reflection.*
- *Look directly into your own eyes and say the following:*

   I am beautiful. I am a force of love.

- *Throw back your shoulders and stand up straight.*
- *Open your heart, still looking into the reflection of your eyes and repeat these words:*

I am healthy.
I am whole.
I am a body of light.
I am love.
I am happy.
I am joy.
I am a walking star.
I am a blessing of the universe.

The following exercise draws on the power of your own individual talisman to help you build self-respect. Pieces of enchanted jewelry, symbolically empowered to draw desirable conditions into the life of the bearer, have had a place in every magical and religious tradition known to humanity. Here, you'll use an old-fashioned key that you can find in a secondhand store. As you carry the key, you will win the respect of those around you.

Exercise Your Spirit:	**The Key to Self Respect**
What you will need:	**A small key (new or old)**
Time:	**Ongoing**

- *Find a key that you like, which you can wear around your neck on a chain or cord or can carry in your pocket.*

- *Wash the key in rose water.*
- *Draw energy into the key by touching it to your heart and to the doors of a number of locations that hold psychic power for you, including:*

  - *A place in which you feel safe*
  - *A place you feel is beautiful*
  - *A place where others gather to enjoy something*
  - *Your favorite store*
  - *Your grocery store*
  - *Your bank*
  - *Your favorite tree*
  - *A flower or the gate to your garden*

- *Wear the key around your neck or carry it in your pocket. From time to time, you might like to hold it close to your heart and know that you have the key to your life. Open the door and live it!*

The key I use is a small antique key I found at a flea market. I took it to many of my favorite stores, one of them being Louis Vuitton, where I put it into the lock of a huge LV steamer trunk. When my flea-market key actually opened the lock, I realized I had a master key! When you absorb the energy of items that you love, magic happens, and I have since found many beautiful Louis Vuitton items coming my way.

The new moon is a good time to begin this ritual again. What is your heart's desire? You have the key!

You Must Feel to Heal

The most important thing I've learned about the emotional body is this: you have to *feel* it to *heal* it. You can talk and analyze all you want, but if you don't feel the pain that has been stored in your emotional body, you're never going to heal it. This is the magic formula to heal old emotional energy: you have to feel it, neutralize it, and replace it. The emotional body sits around the physical body like a cup or a chalice, full of all the emotions and experiences that have accumulated over the years. This cup is always attracting more of what's already in it, so if you're angry, you're going to attract more anger. The good news is that we're all here to heal; the universe always leads you to the healing you need. Whatever your issue, you're eventually going to be pushed into more and more of it, to the point where you have to deal with it. So you might as well go ahead and feel all those emotions you've stored up. Doing so will accelerate the process of dealing with these emotions so your magic can lead you to the life you really want.

The next few exercises can help you feel what you need to feel to clear the wounds of the past from your emotional body and your heart. If the emotional body is not cleaned out, the pain won't go away; it will just sit there, getting in the way of your ability to listen to your heart. A major part of my healing practice is helping people to get into their heart to find safe and healthy ways to express their feelings. We'll do some of that together in the following exercises—crying, getting angry, and even laughing to help you get unstuck and get your life moving again. The whole range of emotions is what makes life so interesting and exciting.

You carry around with you all the emotions you've experienced. Every thought, every feeling that you have is in your energy field; you bring your unhealed emotional issues with you everywhere you go. If you carry around a lot of sadness, everyone you come into contact with will know it: they'll feel the sadness too.

Sadness is often just stored anger. We're conditioned to feel that it's more acceptable to be sad than to be angry, so we suppress our anger by expressing it as sadness. This deflection may feel healthy, but it's actually quite dangerous, because stored anger can take a toll on both your physical and your emotional health.

We can cleanse our sadness through crying. Crying is akin to a rebirth. It's completely natural, not something you have to learn how to do; remember, the first thing a baby does when it's born is cry. Whenever you start to cry, you become unfrozen, vulnerable, and completely in the moment. It shakes something off your energy field to cry. Think about how fresh and clean someone looks after they really feel their emotions and have a good cry: they look reborn, like a garden after a rainstorm. One day my client Janice came in looking especially soft and radiant, and when I told her how pretty she looked, she responded that she had been crying nonstop the last two days. "Everywhere I go, someone gives me a compliment," she said. "I've never met so many men!"

I think of the word *emotion* as meaning "energy in motion," a reminder of these gifts of emotions we've been given to feel and cleanse and flow with life. It's rare that my clients don't cry when we discuss their lives, their tears serving as a healing reaction to the truth. Some people just sit down and start crying! Crying is a sign that you're not in control, and giving up control is necessary for emotional healing. It is sometimes awkward for men, who are not accustomed to crying, but if you don't cry, the energy layers that surround you become hardened. Your life becomes dry and brittle, because it has no tears in it to give it shape. Just as water can turn hard ground to clay that we can mold, our tears can lend shape to our lives.

My gift of sight includes medical intuitive abilities that allow me to see physical changes and occurrences that are invisible to others. As a result, one night I cried so hard that I was able to see steam come out of my heart. That was the evening that I realized I still had more tears to let out over the death of my dearest friend several years earlier. The experience taught me that my tears were covering up more pain than I ever imagined. So don't stop and analyze crying, just allow it to happen. Shortly after my cry, I met my future husband. All those tears opened up my heart, and I was ready to receive love once again.

When you allow yourself to cry, you drop your old masks and lose your identity as a sufferer. The tears you shed in the following exercise will unburden you of years of sadness. You will become more vulnerable, yet you will also lose the need to be in control; you'll feel freer and more spontaneous—and yes, more childlike. Remember the secret to healing your emotions: feel, neutralize, replace.

Exercise Your Spirit:	**Pity Party**
What you will need:	**A timer, lavender soap, scrub brush, music you love**
Time:	**Two hours**

- *Set the timer for one hour and give yourself permission to cry.*
- *Feel it. Sometimes it helps to write a letter to someone that you must never send—a letter filled with all the meaningful things you wish you had said and want to get out of your system.*
- *Let all the sadness you have carried over the years come out.*
- *After the timer goes off, shower off with lavender soap and a scrub brush. Neutralize your sadness. (Lavender heals and balances the emotions.)*
- *After your shower, put on some music that you love and dance for an hour, moving your hands in the sign of infinity (the number 8 on its side). The infinity sign is in our DNA, just waiting to be released. Let go of all limitations. This release replaces the anger with a peaceful experience.*
- *Pour yourself a tall glass of water and hold the water next to your heart.*
- *See yourself truly happy and at peace.*
- *Drink the water at your leisure during the day and give thanks.*

Feeling Anger

Now we get to the part that many people find difficult: feeling the anger that may have accumulated over the years. Anger is a very natural emotion if we feel it, express it, and release it. The problem is that we're trained not to feel anger: we're conditioned to be nice. So instead of feeling anger, we suppress it; we store it rather than feel it. Feeling anger is healthy, but storing anger is deadly.

I've only met a few people in my life who did not have at least some stored anger. When I see anger clairvoyantly, it looks like a very hard shell around the body, much like armor. It has its own distinct shade of smoky, grayish brown. Sounds ugly, doesn't it? Each time you get angry, this armored shell cracks and scar tissue of emotion builds up around you. Eventually you're encased in a layer of crustlike armor that stops other things from entering. You may think you're protecting yourself, but you're actually shielding yourself from love. Anger puts up a wall around you and your experience of life. You can't really be loved completely if you're surrounded by that wall. You can have relationships, but you can't really have intimacy.

You don't have to be clairvoyant to see the anger that some people have stored: it shows up on the physical level as well. I am sure you can just look at certain people and see in their faces that they carry around a lot of anger. You can also see that their light is hidden. As you can imagine, the thicker the armor you surround yourself with, the harder it is to radiate joy. Your heart—your lantern—can be lost behind a wall of stored anger.

My client Lydia's anger was evident to me in our very first session. As I looked at her energy field, I could see the layers of crusty anger that were stored on her face and on her lower abdomen. I suggested that she had some anger that needed to be healed, but she adamantly refused to acknowledge it. About halfway through the session she told me that she wanted to get some photos from her car for me to see. When she went outside, I locked the door and sat in a chair very visible to the outside. She knocked, but I did not respond. She banged on the door and yelled until she finally broke down in tears. After a few minutes I opened the door and brought her inside to process her pain. She had a powerful *aha!* moment, realizing that she had been angry a long time, even as she remained detached from her feelings; afterward she was finally able to create real relationships. Lydia has never forgotten this crazy act that my intuition led me to do. Every year she needlepoints me a beautiful pillow thanking me for changing her life.

Sometimes people are afraid of their anger. My client Kata was angry about the fact that she was afraid to speak up because she had gotten in trouble speaking up when she was little. Her anger grew like a money market account that just kept collecting and collecting. Meanwhile she kept attracting angry men into her life, and it was these men's anger that she always wanted to talk about—never her own. As she worked with the exercises of this key, however, Kata realized that focusing on the anger of those around her made it easy to overlook the effect her own anger was having on her life. She can now see how much of her family's anger she absorbed when she was young, and she is learning a lot about how to express the feelings she had been afraid to communicate before.

The following exercise has helped many other clients achieve real breakthroughs as they let go of their stored-up anger. Over and over I've heard people say what a difference the exercise has made in their lives. They can feel it, and I can see it too! Sometimes I don't even recognize them after they've done it, they look so different.

Exercise Your Spirit: **Anger Release**
What you will need: **A timer, an 18-inch**
length of rubber
plumbing hose from

Time:

the hardware store, an
old phone book,
lavender soap, a bath
brush, music you love
90 minutes

Part One: Feeling the Anger

- *Gather your equipment in a place where you can be comfortably alone and make noise.*
- *Set the timer for thirty minutes.*
- *Get on your knees. (This position opens up your body, allowing all the energy to move through your entire physical body; this is why this position has long been used for prayer.)*
- *Bring to mind a person or situation that you feel frustrated or angry about.*
- *Say what you really wanted to say at that time (It may be as simple as NO! or Listen to me!).*
- *Hit the phone book with the rubber hose as you say it again and again.*
- *Keep beating the phone book as you speak—or yell— until the timer goes off.*
- *Give yourself permission to let go and feel and release this old poison.*

Part Two: Neutralizing the Anger

- *Wash away the released anger in a shower, using the brush to scrub your body with the lavender soap.*

Part Three: Replacing the Anger with Peace

- *When you are clean, dry, and dressed, spend one hour (twice the amount of time you spend expressing your anger) dancing to music that you love. Again use the infinity sign to release all limitations.*
- *See yourself as free from the past.*
- *Allow the space created in your body by the release of your anger to be replaced with love.*

Imagine how you'll feel when you let go of all those years of anger! I think the most powerful change I have seen people make occurs when they express and replace their anger. But you must replace it! That's why part three of the exercise is so important. When you clean out a drawer, you must organize and refill it immediately, or it will soon be overflowing with junk. Your emotional body works the same way. Releasing your anger creates a vacuum in your energy field, and something has to take its place. You must intentionally replace your anger with love, or the anger will sink back into the body.

The anger exercise can feel uncomfortable to do, but I've never met anyone who didn't say that doing it made a tremendous difference in his or her life. I've had many people do it in front of me, which always makes me feel really blessed: it takes a lot of trust to expose your vulnerability in front of someone else like that. But I don't have to be there for it to work for you! My client Maria did most of her work with me by telephone, so she did the exercise several times at home, on her own. After serving as the president of a corporation for fourteen years, she was laid off at the age of forty-five when the company was sold. Maria's career had truly been her life—she was divorced, had no relationship, and her two children had left home to go to college—so she was in a great deal of pain.

I told Maria that she needed to feel her feelings and allow them to run their course, and I gave her the sadness and anger exercises to do. Three weeks later she called and said she felt lighter and happier, but I still heard in her voice a need for her to continue, so I suggested that she keep going. The next time I saw her, when I was visiting her area, it had been almost a year since our last face-to-face visit. I couldn't believe it was the same person when she walked in. She looked fantastic! She had moved beyond her anger, realizing that what had happened to her was the universe's way of moving her toward her dream: she had lined up investors, started her own company, and hired a lot of her former employees, who had jumped ship to come to work for her.

Maria did the exercises several times to achieve so much change; it takes a lot of energy to start your life over in your mid-forties, and the results Maria has manifested are testament to the amount of effort she put in. Instead of giving everything to a company, she's now giving it back to herself, and her life is really flourishing.

Have a Good Laugh

Feeling your sadness and your anger will also enhance your ability to laugh. If you allow yourself to really cry, you will be able to laugh more freely. Laughter that has no tears has a superficial quality, a falseness to it. If you give yourself permission to dissolve into your anger and your tears, a totally different quality of beautiful, bell-like laughter will arise from you.

I love laughter, unless it is used to avoid feeling your feelings.

It's not as natural as crying: after all, babies don't come into the world laughing. Still, laughter and crying are interlinked and can help you relieve your tension. Once in a while, if you have a deep laugh from your very roots, you will feel a great boost of energy, a fresh vitality to move into your magic. Laughter can help you shake off a shield you don't know you're carrying.

Laughter can also provide a less intimidating alternative to the anger release exercise. It's not always as effective, but there's a laughing meditation exercise that the ancient Hawaiians did that can be very healing. I used to do it with my kids and pretty soon we'd all be laughing until our stomachs hurt. Try it; it's intoxicating!

Exercise Your Spirit:	**Laughing Meditation**
What you will need:	**You**
Time:	**10 minutes**

- *Force yourself to laugh.*
- *Keep laughing until your forced laughter becomes real. Believe me, it will happen.*
- *Continue laughing for ten minutes.*
- *Enjoy the looseness that it brings to your body.*
- *Take a hot bath and allow the cells in your physical body to expand.*

Laughter can be as sacred as prayer. Years ago a friend took me to meet a Tibetan monk while we were traveling to Santa Fe, New Mexico. I was very excited, as I had read a lot of Tibetan philosophy, and I had never met a Tibetan holy man. We visited a temple that was just being completed, and when the beautiful spiritual man opened the door, he started coughing and told us he was suffering from a cold. All day I had been quiet and very contemplative, but something happened to me, and all of a sudden I found myself becoming a clown. I was very playful and silly. The monk spent the whole time laughing. By the end of the visit he had stopped coughing and was on the road to recovery. Laughter can be so healing, and if you have to heal—which we all do—you might as well make it fun!

Forgiveness Comes from the Heart

As we let go of our anger, our hearts call us into forgiveness. Forgiveness is the key to happiness. But forgiveness doesn't come from the mind, and it isn't expressed in words. True forgiveness can come only from the heart. If you haven't forgiven, it's hard to find the real joy in your life, because your blame is always there as a barrier separating you from other people, from your life, even from yourself.

There can be no real forgiveness if you have not healed the feelings from the past. I think it's an ongoing challenge for each of us to continue to forgive what life has given us and what we have created in our lives. *To forgive* means to "give completely" so we have to go back and view ourselves as we did before our wounds happened—such as at that point in childhood when we first started to think that we weren't good enough or weren't loved enough.

Wade was living in San Francisco when he learned that his mother in Kentucky had been diagnosed with lung cancer. Raised from the age of seven by his father after his parents' divorce, Wade had never been very close to his mother but had always wanted a closer relationship with her. At the age of thirty-two, he wanted to move back to Kentucky and care for his mother, but he was afraid of giving up his life in the Bay Area. His head told him no, giving him many reasons to stay, but his heart was shouting *MOVE!* Wade worked very hard to quiet his mind and listen to his heart, and he decided to move back to Kentucky and work from his mother's house. Wade's desire to love and be loved by his mother illuminated the darkness of his fears, and he really got to know his mother as he cared for her in her final days. Wade has no regrets about his decision, as he feels that the closeness and joy that resulted from the experience of caring for his mother were more than worth the sacrifice. In fact, Wade not only found that he enjoyed Kentucky but met a wonderful woman who worked at his mother's hospital. His life now has new direction—all because he was able to forgive his mother and heal his childhood wound.

Many people come to me looking for forgiveness. We grow when we can be forgiven; that's what the whole Catholic idea of weekly confession is about. Now many people seek that forgiveness elsewhere, from therapists or spiritual advisers. When a client can reveal his darkest secrets to me, he doesn't have to carry them around anymore. It's a huge relief. And when I can provide that for others, I also feel forgiven—that wonderful feeling of being open, vulnerable, and completely alive.

We can be far more forgiving of others if we can forgive ourselves. But forgiveness is not a onetime thing. You can heal today and then you have to heal again tomorrow. Life is a continual journey of forgiving, living, loving, and forgiving.

The next exercise focuses this effort on a single week. I first gave it to a woman named Heather, who was clinging so tenaciously to the pain in her past that she spent her entire first session talking nonstop. At the close of the hour, having had no chance to give any insight to her, I told her to listen to the tape of our session seven times and do the following exercise.

Exercise Your Spirit:	**Seven Photos**
What you will need:	**Seven pictures of yourself**
Time:	**One week**

- *Take seven photos of yourself from your photo gallery, from infancy to present day.*
- *Each day for a week, take one picture out and keep it with you all day.*
- *Embrace that version of you.*
- *In your mind's eye, see the you of today hugging the you of the photograph.*

I never heard from Heather again, but nine months later a woman came in and said she wanted the exercise that her friend Heather said had changed her life. This second woman already knew all the instructions but still felt she needed me to tell her to do it. I told her she did not need my permission to forgive herself!

It is often easier to talk about forgiveness than to practice it. My client Mary Ellen came to me very upset that her teenaged nephew had left a big mess in her apartment after coming to stay there. She had let him know how angry she was, and after he apologized, she told him she forgave him. I explained that to be true to the meaning of forgiveness—to give completely—she would need to give her nephew the key to her apartment the next time he came to L.A. She knew when I told her this that she had not yet truly forgiven him! She needed to do the anger exercise before she could move forward.

The next time her nephew came, after she had done the anger release work, Mary Ellen once again gave him the key to her apartment. This time he felt empowered and avoided making the same mistake. Mary Ellen's act of forgiveness made it possible for them to mend their relationship, to shed any anger between them. Her offering him the key was a huge sign of trust that he had learned his lesson—but it was an even bigger sign that she had learned her lesson of forgiveness.

The more you love yourself and forgive yourself, the more prepared you are to receive, to listen to your heart. As soon as your heart is clean, you just naturally begin to play and listen. You'll feel that tingle in your body that you get when you're listening. You've felt it before—like when you have a hunch that turns out to be true. It makes you feel special to open up and listen. You feel useful and connected. It's the feeling of being connected to everything in the universe.

The next exercise is one of the most powerful I know of for preparing the heart to receive and for looking at life through a clean lens.

Exercise Your Spirit:	Preparing to Receive
What you will need:	You
Time:	15 minutes

- *Close your eyes and take some deep breaths, filling your lungs completely.*
- *Release your breath very slowly, as if blowing through a straw.*
- *Bring into your mind a time in your past when you felt good about how you looked.*
- *Make a fist with your right hand and press into your heart as you think of this memory. Hold the pressure to the count of three.*
- *Now take a deep breath and release.*
- *Remember a time you received a compliment from someone.*
- *Press your right fist into your heart as you think of this memory. Hold the pressure to the count of three.*
- *Now take a deep breath and release.*
- *Remember a time when you received a gift from someone.*
- *Press your right fist into your heart as you think of this memory. Hold the pressure to the count of three.*
- *Take another deep breath and release.*
- *Remember a time when you received something you really wanted (perhaps as a child, on your birthday or at a holiday).*
- *Press your right fist into your heart as you think of this memory. Again hold the pressure to the count of three.*
- *Take another deep breath and release.*
- *Think of a time when you had an intuitive hunch (perhaps you suddenly thought about someone and then soon afterward ran into or heard from that person).*

- *Press your right fist into your heart as you think of this memory.*
- *Take a deep breath and release.*

For the next seven days, concentrate on receiving. When you receive something, breathe and put your fist into your heart and press. When someone gives you a compliment, breathe before you say "thank you." Feel your connection with spirit. As you receive the gifts that are before you, you will begin to receive your love for yourself.

Now It Is Time to Receive

All the desires of your heart are within reach. You have within you all that you need to fulfill your desires and create the life you really want. Know that each time you have a deep longing, you are planting a seed. Think of something that you would like to create in your life right now, and join me in this exercise.

Exercise Your Spirit:	**Sky Dreams**
What you will need:	**7 sheets of paper**
Time:	**Ongoing**

- *Take out your notebook and go to the page where you wrote about looking into the sky for a cloud.*
- *Visualize the shape you saw in your mind's eye, seeing it very clearly in your mind.*
- *Think of something that you desire very much.*

- *Imagine that you are painting that symbol on seven parts of your body, each time giving yourself permission to receive what you desire.*
- *Take out seven pieces of paper and draw or paint the symbol on each one.*
- *Put these seven drawings or paintings up in the power places of your life, places that you encounter ever day:*

  1. *wherever you look when you wake up in the morning*
  2. *on your mirror*
  3. *on your fridge*
  4. *in your car*
  5. *on your computer*
  6. *in your wallet*
  7. *on the door of your bedroom*

- *Leave them up until you receive what you want.*

Can it actually change your life to have paper icons posted all around? Every time you see the symbol, you will be reminded that you can receive what you want. At first you might think that they will disappear, the way fortune cookie fortunes stuck to the refrigerator seem to become invisible after a couple of days. But symbols go into the unconscious faster than words; the image bypasses the intellect. So every time those little emblems catch your eye, they will trigger your imagination. Some days you will see your personal symbol everywhere! Soon after you put them up, odd coincidences will start happening and then multiplying.

When you draw a personal symbol that comes from—and

speaks to—your unconscious, and you keep seeing it in different places within your reality, something shifts in your brain and you begin to see and feel your life differently. I have countless many letters from people saying that this simple exercise changed their lives.

After you have cleansed your emotional body, you are ready to learn how to use your will. You have the energy of the universe at your fingertips. The next key will teach you how to harness that energy to create magic with power and focus. So be it.

CHAPTER 4

KEY 4: Your Will Is Your Wand

What matters is not the length of the wand,
but the magic in the stick.

—ANONYMOUS

Now that you are in touch with your magic, it is time to find your wand. From ancient alchemists to Harry Potter, magi have long been pictured wielding their magic wands. The wand is the most important aid in magic, the instrument of the magus's unique and absolute power. Above all, the magic wand is a symbol of the will, the capacity to influence the world and bring dreams to reality. Wouldn't you love to have an actual wand that you could hold in your hand to create even greater magic? Your wand is waiting and ready to be put to use. But you must find the will inside you before you can use it to charge your wand.

Will is something that we all have the capacity to develop. The exercises in Key Four will teach you how to appreciate and strengthen your personal will to exert your influence in the world. You will then learn how to create a wand that serves as an extension and instrument of your unique will. Most important, you'll see that you can use your will the way a magus uses a wand—to create magic in your life and the lives of others.

Understanding will is about understanding energy. You are operating on pure energy, and your will is a focus of this energy. To strengthen and direct your will, you'll need to know more about the human energy system and the universal laws that govern it. This knowledge will bring you benefits that are both practical and profound. Exploring your energy system will help you heal any separation between your higher and lower selves and enable you to transform destructive thoughts or emotional patterns. When you strengthen your will, you find out who you truly are, unlocking forgotten wisdom to increase your personal power and build your self-esteem. Working with this knowledge will bring you into harmony with the universe and activate your intuition, the guidance of the soul that can lead you to your magical life. It will also teach you how to use your twelve senses (listed on pp. 00–00) to access inner knowledge and merge with the universal flow so you may intuitively and gracefully live your life. Doesn't that sound just good enough to be true?

The will is associated with the fire element. Fire holds mystery and danger in its flame; in moderation, fire can be useful—keeping us warm, cooking our food—but out of control it is devastating. In some situations the element may be too dangerous to use for magical purposes, so you can substitute something red, like a lightbulb, lampshade, or bedspread. Join me in inviting fire to be a part of our journey.

Exercise Your Spirit: Fire Blessing
What you will need: A fireplace or candle
Time: 10–15 minutes

- *Light a fire in the fireplace or light a candle and chant this call to the fire element:*

Oh Great Fire:
Burn down all the walls and self-made doors
Help me seek my soul and more

Guide me with a simple flash
Lightning come and make me dance

Heal my body, mind, and soul
Bring me light and make me bold

Please, hot fire, I need your light
Bring my dreams into my sight

- *Now take the list of faults you made in your personal inventory in the last chapter and burn it in the fireplace or in another safe, contained place.*
- *Honor the warmth of the sun, the electricity you use to live your life, the fire in someone's eyes, and give thanks.*

Have you ever tried to break a harmful habit? We all know that it's easier to say you're going to end a habit than it is to actually do it. As you strengthen the fire element within, you will be able to break habits quickly and cleanly. You can think all you want about ridding yourself of a habit, but if you keep engaging in the undesired behavior, you'll still be stuck in it. To break a habit, you have to know that you have the desire and ability to change your behavior. Feel the difference: Say out loud, 'I can change.' Now say, 'I will change.' Which sounds stronger? You must start acting in a different way. It might be hard at first, but if you keep on acting in this new way, the action becomes easier and easier until it's absolutely natural. My client Patrick had been smoking since he was fifteen years old when he started working with the Seven Keys. At the age of thirty-four, he was finally ready to quit. It was interesting to watch him develop his will, and he actually had an easy time quitting. His friends did not think he could do it. He willed it to be.

That's the difference between the mind and the will. The mind might tell you that you "should" break a habit, or that you're going to change your behavior, but your will is what actually moves you to action. The mind makes noise but the will gets results. That's why we first had to learn to silence the mind before we could concentrate on focusing the will. Throughout the ages, spiritual writings have devised many practices to quiet the mind and strengthen the will. Take the example of repeated, ritualized prayer: if you keep on praying with your lips, sooner or later you will one day find yourself praying with your heart. Through action and repetition, the mind is silenced and the will engages the heart.

The ancients who developed the sacred science of magic identified will, or volition, as one of the four fundamental qualities that must be inherent in each magus. Knowledge, daring, silence, and volition are regarded as the four pillars of a magical life, without which nothing can be achieved in holy magic. The first three qualities are achieved by working with the first three keys: by expecting magic, we are open to knowledge; by shedding fear, we are un-afraid of sacrifice or hindrances; by quieting the mind, we embrace silence. The final pillar, volition, is obtained through toughness, patience, and perseverance; if you earnestly follow the path to wisdom rather than set out simply to satisfy your curiosity, you will possess unshakable will.

When someone demonstrates a will that strong, we say that person has backbone. Not surprisingly, the backbone is the part of the body that represents the will and the fire element inside of you. Your will is housed in your spine, which also serves as the foundation of your energy system. As you'll see, the spine is where you find your *chakras,* the distribution centers for directing the flow of divine energy throughout your physical body. Think of your spine as your internal wand—the channel for your natural energy and for the will you use to project it onto the world. Let's start the process of getting in touch with your inner wand with a simple stretch to straighten and strengthen your spine.

Exercise Your Spirit:	**Stretch Your Inner Wand**
What you will need:	**You**
Time:	**15–20 minutes**

- *Stand with your feet shoulder-width apart, knees bent and arms relaxed.*
- *Tuck your chin into your chest and slowly roll down until your hands reach the floor. Make sure your knees are soft, not locked.*
- *Let your body hang loosely forward from your hips.*

- *Hold for ten seconds.*
- *Slowly roll up to an upright position, one vertebra at a time.*
- *Repeat four times.*
- *Be sure to move slowly; you'll get maximum benefit if you stretch into the exercise.*
- *Variation: As you get stronger and your leg muscles lengthen, bend your knees a little less. Also, try touching your fingertips and even the palms of your hands to the floor.*

The true magus tones downs his strength with humility, never calling attention to his power. When you begin to use your magic wand, you become a servant of the universe, so you must humbly honor and respect the universe's governing principles. Observing the sunset, the stars at night, the four seasons, the waxing and waning moon, we cannot deny the perfect design and order of the universe; everything from the biggest planet to the smallest atom follows precise laws of nature. We are beings of energy, and energy is governed by universal laws and principles. To prepare for your magical powers and step into your magical life, you must learn how to work with the universal laws. There are four divine laws that rule this world and all of us that are alive within it: the Laws of Energy, Polarity, Cause and Effect, and Grace.

The Law of Energy: Energy is the force of the universe. Everything on this planet, including you and me, is made up of particles of energy. We are all made up of the same material. This means that we are all linked—to the universe and to each other. The Law of Energy reminds us that we are all one, and that each one of us can influence the harmony of the world and everyone in it. As you go about your day, look at the world around you and repeat this affirmation: *I am one with all that is.*

The Law of Polarity: The rose will either delight you with its fragrance or cut you with its thorns. Our world is filled with opposites—black and white, good and evil, light and dark, positive and negative—so there's no point in judging these differences or pretending that they don't exist. Remember that whatever you see in others is actually within you. Where your attention goes, your energy flows, so the Law of Polarity compels you to understand all sides of yourself and focus on where you want your life to go. It's easier to take ownership of your life when things go well, but when we encounter something "bad," we often want to think that it "happened" to us. The truth is that we have the capacity to create both good and bad, and we have more power to draw the positive when we accept that fact. When you find that you are about to judge, repeat this affirmation of your desire to create only good: *I am a source of good at all times.*

The Law of Cause and Effect: Remember the ancient proverb, "Whatsoever a man soweth, that shall he also reap." Every deed proceeds from a cause, and each cause sets free a corresponding effect. You've probably heard this principle referred to as karma; you might have also heard that karma comes back to you in seven days, seven weeks, seven months, or seven years. As you accelerate your life, however, it could be more like seven hours, seven minutes, or seven seconds—all the more reason to honor the Law of Cause and Effect. Remember that karma can be either bad or good: for every good deed we do, we receive back ten times. When you are tempted to disregard your heart and do something other than what you know is in your highest good, repeat this affirmation: *All that I give comes back to me.*

The Law of Grace: We receive grace by recognizing ourselves in another person, which we do through forgiveness, playfulness, and most especially love. Expressing unconditional love will bring many blessings to you and inspire you to

- *recognize and accept love as your true nature;*
- *be loving, gentle, and respectful toward others in your thoughts, words, and actions;*
- *surrender your ego to others;*
- *honor the importance of your relationships with others;*
- *be centered and connected to your inner source;*
- *serve and support others in their personal and spiritual growth;*
- *keep communications open and keep love conscious, active, and present.*

Grace can help us heal and grow together; think of someone or a situation that needs healing and use this affirmation: *With my forgiveness, I receive grace.*

Energy Moves Us

If I could see you right now, I would see energy moving in a spiral formation in many beautiful colors all around you. My gift of sight enables me to see clearly how energy works within and around all of us. Imagine that you are a lightbulb emanating waves of vibrant color that move into and out of your body. Your body, mind, emotions, and soul are all energy. Some forms of energy operate at frequencies that make them less visible than others. As a clairvoyant, however, I can by second nature see the human energy system and its three primary components: the ray, our portal to the source of divine light; the aura, the energy that moves through our bodies; and the chakras, the wheels that move the energy around. By studying people's energy systems, I can learn a lot about why they're here, where they are in their journey, and how far they are likely to go. The more you know about your own energy system, the better you'll be able to find your magic and use it in the world.

The ray is the pure energy that comes into the body through the crown of your head to connect you to the divine source of light. God gives each of us different gifts and qualities to bring to earth, and these gifts and qualities have different colors. The unique combination of gifts that you have come to earth to share and develop is expressed in the color makeup of your ray; if you have been sent to earth to have a strong body and work on your mind and spirit, for example, your ray will look different from the ray of an individual whose spirit is strong but who needs to work on mind and body.

Knowing the colors of your ray can help you understand the energy you were born with—the strengths you might want to develop and the possible challenges you might want to look out for. The colors described below can be combined in an infinite number of variations; as you read about the qualities of each color, you will probably be able to determine which colors are in your ray.

1. Yellow ray: Known for their logic, accuracy, tolerance, and patience, yellow ray people love facts. They have active minds that they use to analyze everything, and they love to read and absorb whatever information they can find in books, magazines, newspapers, and so on. They also have very good gut-level intuition—if they can keep their mind out of the way! Motivated to find answers to every question, yellow ray people can generally offer clear explanations of things, but their presentation often lacks heart or emotion. They make excellent researchers and accountants. They can also tend to be very materialistic—more than any of the other rays. I find that yellow ray people often have difficulty relaxing or relating to people in a spontaneous way and frequently have problems with migraine headaches or arthritis. I always suggest meditation and relaxation methods to help give them greater flexibility of mind.

2. Pink ray: This ray produces evangelical people who are here to raise the consciousness of mankind through service. Their qualities are devotion, love, and loyalty. I call this the angelic ray, because such people will always find a cause to which they can be totally devoted. They are very in tune with themselves and generally do not take advice from others. They are romantic, emotional, and sentimental, and they get grumpy if they are misunderstood. Children and animals love this energy and are visibly responsive to it. Tender and gullible, the pink rays often teach in too soft a manner, and they frequently suffer from various abdominal problems.

3. Orange ray: Orange ray people are the peacekeepers; their main quality is harmony. This ray is very sensitive and emotional. Orange rays are the most loyal of all the rays and have difficulty letting go of relationships; they would generally rather say "perhaps" than tell someone no. People tell them everything, as they are natural counselors or healers. They tend to self-sacrifice and often have martyr issues to work through—as well as intestinal congestion, lower back weakness, and weight issues. More than any other ray, these people want and need harmony. Some can become psychic sponges and soak in other people's feelings. They tend to like to be in the middle of things, including other people's problems; luckily they seem to be catalysts to finding resolutions. Jacks-of-all-trades, orange ray people are often masters of none.

4. Blue ray: I call this ray the messenger ray. Blue ray people are very sensitive to preconscious sources of information, which can make them great teachers and healers. Their qualities are universal love, wisdom, insight, and intuition. Wisdom is more than intellectual knowledge; it is the knowledge gained by experiencing something through mind, body, and soul—by being it, doing it, and living it. Because they must live their lessons, blue ray people seem to go through a lot of trial and error. They are witty and verbal and are natural communicators who thrive on working with people. They have a deep need to express themselves through writing, speaking, singing, or having a career in some area of the media. They tend to get skin ailments and have problems with the liver or gall bladder.

5. Green ray: Green ray people love to grow things; they have the "green thumb." Their qualities are comprehension, healing, nurturing, tact, and impartiality. They love nature and need to be in a natural environment. They often have trouble being in crowds and can seem a bit aloof, even having a cooling effect when they enter a room. Green rays are creative, innovative people, but they are not always as good at implementing their ideas. They are generally introverted and prefer to write what they feel and think rather than speak about it. They have weakness in the kidneys and the bladder and often have poor circulation.

6. Purple ray: With qualities of precision, grace, dignity, and nobility, these individuals have a noble bearing. They love ceremony, ritual, and power. Purple ray people are like suns, independent and self-sufficient. They need a lot of freedom to act and express themselves, which often means working alone. They love the arts and are attracted to beauty. I find that they are often insecure, having felt isolated or misunderstood for much of their lives. They grasp things as a whole and are not interested in the details of the picture. They suffer nervous system imbalances and disorders of the adrenal glands.

7. Red ray: These are strong-willed people who are natural and courageous leaders. They seem to be very drawn to power and influence. Often they have talents in so many areas that they have trouble choosing their direction, but when they do, they can become leaders in the highest sense of the word, using their power for the good of all. In relationships, they guide and direct with little softness or romance in their manner. They are never gentle people and are often at their best under adversity. They are prone to developing weakness in their hearts, hips, and legs.

Once I've seen the colors of a person's ray, I look at what's going on in their aura. Where the ray shows your potential, the aura reveals your experience; think of the ray as the input and the aura as the output. The aura has many layers, and it changes every fraction of a second, shifting with each thought or feeling. If you were speaking to me now, I would be able to tell from the changes in your aura whether you were communicating from your heart or from your head, whether you were speaking your own truth or saying something you read or were told. Your aura would reveal pieces of your life and show me where energy is moving and where it is stagnant, information I could use to create a road map to help you understand your past and move you toward a brighter future.

It takes a lot of experience and trust to see and interpret all the information that is contained in the many layers of the aura. But you don't have to be a clairvoyant just to see people's auras, and this simple exercise will help you begin to see your own. I've taught it in many classes, and almost everyone begins to see their aura under the correct circumstances. At first it's very subtle, or even invisible to you, but with practice you will see it.

Exercise Your Spirit:	**See Your Aura**
What you will need:	**A mirror**
Time:	**Ongoing**

- *Take a hot bath or shower and dry off.*
- *Light a candle and turn out the lights.*
- *Stand naked in front of a full-length mirror.*
- *Try to see the light around your body. Start above the crown of the head, then place your hand in front of you and look at the outline of the hand. The physical*

aura is an ice blue color, which is surrounded by a golden yellow protective shield.

- *Relax your eyes. Do not strain. Ask to see and let it happen. The secret is not to see your physical body, so you must allow yourself to become luminous. Experience expansion. As you breathe out, your aura expands, and as you breathe in, it contracts. You are like a pulsating star!*
- *Don't pay attention to your physical shape, just focus on the light around the form.*
- *Continue looking for ten to fifteen minutes.*
- *Keep trying once a week until you can see the light around your body. You might need three weeks, and you might need three months. Some people say they "sense" their aura more than they actually see it. Just decide it's possible and keep trying!*

As revealing as a person's ray and aura can be, I find that I learn the most about a person by focusing on their chakra system. *Chakra* is the ancient Sanskrit word for "wheel," which is a good description of how chakras operate: they turn like wheels to distribute energy throughout the body. Indian Yogis were the first to write about the human body's seven chakras. Though most texts still speak of only seven chakras, I see twelve that influence and reflect our lives, each one calibrated to pick up a certain range of energies relating to different areas of our lives.

Do you want to feel more comfortable and powerful in your body and in your life than ever before? Learning about your chakras will enable you to draw on your energy system to strengthen your will and enlighten both your physical and emotional bodies. On a clairvoyant level, the chakras look like small, spinning CDs that receive and send out energy the way radio transmitters or satellites handle information. Think of the chakras as distribution centers: as energy comes into the body, the chakras send it to the organs and out into the aura. Just as there are twelve hours on the clock, twelve months in the year, and twelve houses in an astrological chart, there are twelve chakras. The seven chakras that are most commonly discussed and written about are on the physical spine, between the base of the spinal column and the top of the head, and the other five are off the body but within the body's field or aura.

Over the years, I've learned that chakras have amazing integrity. The chakras hold no secrets or deceptions but reflect exactly what is going on in the body and give responses that are quick, spontaneous, and honest. Once one chakra responds, all the others do in turn, without delay. If someone is not in harmony with himself, the chakras show it.

Your chakras will keep channeling your life force as long as you're alive. But fear, anger, past emotional trauma, and low self-esteem can damage your chakras. When chakras are damaged, energy flows through the body more slowly, lowering the body's overall health. Fortunately, you can heal your chakras with love and joy, as well as with techniques that are specific to each chakra; the more you know about your chakras and their attributes, the easier it is to keep them moving and healthy.

As you'll see, each chakra relates to a specific area of your life; take note of the areas that you want to work on, and you'll get a good idea of which chakras you might want to begin healing first. When you begin to open and align your chakras, you may feel your metabolism speed up, or you may notice that you are releasing energy blocks in your mind and body. And the more work you do, the better your energy flows, filling your body with light and accelerating your progress toward your magical life.

The **first chakra,** or root chakra, transmits your bond with the earth; located at your tailbone at the base of your spine, it relates to feeling physically and emotionally comfortable. If your first chakra is open, you feel grounded, stable, and secure—present in the moment and connected to your physical body. Expressions like "on firm ground" or "back on your feet again" suggest an open root chakra. If you tend to feel nervous or fearful, your root chakra is probably underactive; if you often get overly materialistic, resist change, or focus obsessively on a need to be secure, your first chakra might be working too hard. The natural color of the first chakra is red.

My client Jackie's mother told me that her daughter had a weight problem, but when Jackie showed up, it was clear that she was far from heavy. Jackie was absolutely beautiful, but her mother's fearful comments had distorted Jackie's self-image so profoundly that she had developed an eating disorder. She felt large and uncomfortable in her own body, a sure sign that her first chakra was closed. After we worked together on her energy field, Jackie began to see how her own beauty had been hidden. She started to blossom and developed a new self-image. Now that she feels safe in her body, Jackie believes that she is a deeply beautiful and valuable woman, and her life reflects it.

The first chakra is closely connected to the sense of smell, so one of the things I asked Jackie to do was bathe in bath salts scented with cedar, which is very grounding. The baths helped Jackie learn to love her body and accept herself. When your root chakra is closed too far, you may actually feel that your feet don't seem to touch the ground. Here's an exercise I've often given to help clients strengthen their connection to the ground.

Exercise Your Spirit: **Find Your Tail**
What you will need: **You**
Time: **5 minutes**

- *Stand up straight and relaxed with your feet shoulder-width apart.*
- *Slightly bend your knees.*
- *Put your pelvis somewhat forward.*
- *Keep your body balanced, so your weight is evenly distributed over the soles of your feet.*
- *Sink your weight downward.*
- *Feel your tail bone at the base of your spine and imagine that you can move it in a clockwise direction. Move it around so it becomes flexible. It is meant to connect you to the security of the earth.*

The **second chakra**, or sacral chakra, is about feelings and sexuality. Located about one inch below the belly button, it transmits energy about dealing with pleasure in all parts of your life. When your sacral chakra is open, your feelings flow freely and can be expressed without your becoming overemotional. You are open to intimacy and sexuality and can be passionate and lively. If you tend to be stiff or unemotional, your second chakra is underactive; you might be closed off to people or hide behind a poker face. If this chakra is overactive, you tend to be emotional all the time, developing unhealthy attachments to people and feeling obsessively sexual. The natural color of the second chakra is orange.

Rick and Eliza had been married for over ten years when they came to me. They really loved each other, but they no longer felt any sexual desire and had simply stopped having sex; they hugged and kissed, but that was that. I could see that both of their second chakras were locked up, as were their throat chakras—not surprising, since sexuality and communication are connected. As it turned out, Eliza felt that Rick didn't spend enough time talking to her about her feelings or sexual needs, and she had shut down.

The sense of taste is associated with the second chakra, so I suggested that in the early evening they have a hot chocolate drink or eat a little chocolate. I also gave them the following exercise.

Exercise Your Spirit:	**Breathing Orange**
What you will need:	**You**
Time:	**10 minutes**

- *Visualize your chakras moving energy out the front and the back of your body, like an hourglass.*
- *Imagine that you can breathe an orange light into your body about one inch below your belly button.*
- *Breathe the orange into the front of your body, and then release the breath as if the orange light is going out the back of your body.*

- *Breathe the orange into the back of your body and out the front of your body.*
- *Breathe the orange light into the front of your body and at the same time breathe it into the back of your body, holding your breath.*
- *Imagine as you hold your breath that you are spinning the chakra as fast as you can.*
- *Then let all the energy release out both the front of your body and the back of your body as you release the breath.*

Within a week Rick and Eliza were making love again, and soon after that, they began to communicate about what had made them stop in the first place. Communication was the key. Often couples do not take time to communicate and therefore lose their sexual electrical spark.

The **third chakra**, or navel chakra, deals with the full range of emotions. The expansion of this chakra brings honesty, integrity, and self-esteem. When the navel chakra is underactive, you tend to be passive, timid, and indecisive; overactivity, on the other hand, can result in aggression. The third chakra is located at the diaphragm, and its natural color is yellow.

Petal came to me to work on her self-esteem. A Yale graduate with a degree in economics, she had left the workforce to care for her two children; once they reached school age, however, her lifelong desire to contribute to society returned. Despite her eagerness to use her skills to help the planet, Petal lacked the confidence to push herself out into the world. We discovered a block in her third chakra, which we set out to strengthen using yellow light, ylang-ylang fragrance, and visualization exercises in which she saw herself powerful and successful. I asked her to see the sun shining out of her diaphragm. She is now organizing a group to stop smoking in public places; more important than that, she is full of passion for her life.

The **fourth chakra** is about love, kindness, and affection. Also known as the heart chakra, it scans the love that comes into your world, and houses the possibility for creating relationships. When the heart chakra is open, you are compassionate and friendly, and you work at making your relationships harmonious. An underactive heart chakra will leave you cold and distant; too much activity, and you'll love for selfish reasons and suffocate people with your affections. The natural color of the fourth chakra is green, and it is located in the center of the chest against the spine.

Jim is a Realtor who gives everything to his clients, working sixty-hour weeks and skipping vacations so he doesn't let them down. He loves his work and puts his whole heart into it—so much so, that he always seems tired and stressed when I see him. He is a giver, not a receiver—buying his clients gifts, giving them part of his commission back. When he came to me, it was immediately obvious that some of the energy in his heart chakra was blocked. Jim had forgotten how to play and have fun, and he needed some tenderness for himself. To teach Jim to relax and open his heart, I asked him to wear green as often as possible and breathe green into his heart. I also suggested that he carry a rose quartz in his pocket and seek out the fragrance of sandalwood, breathing it in and even bathing in it. The sense of touch really helps to heal the heart, so I asked him to get regular massages. All of these little measures eventually helped: as I write this, Jim is on the first vacation he has taken as long as I've known him, traveling to Hawaii. I asked him to let the world touch him while he's there.

Exercise Your Spirit:	**Open Your Heart to Yourself**
What you will need:	**You**
Time:	**Ongoing**

- *Breathe a deep green light into the center of your chest.*
- *Fill up your chest with this rich green color*
- *As you breathe it out, say,* I love you . . , *completing the statement with your full name.*
- *Repeat four times.*

The **fifth chakra**, or throat chakra, concerns expression; located at the base of the throat, it helps us fulfill ourselves through the expression of our natural talents. An open throat chakra means that a person has no trouble with self-expression; when it's underactive, the individual may be shy or untalkative, while the reverse holds true when it's overactive. Not speaking the truth can suppress its activity; not listening can be a sign of too much activity. The natural color of the throat chakra is blue.

Randy walked into my office full of fear and barely able to talk about her life. Feeling unchallenged and restricted by her city-planning job, she wanted something more but couldn't say what; in fact, it was clear from the high pitch of her voice that she was not speaking from the depth of her body. I noticed that Randy's throat chakra was stuck in the past, so we talked about her family. She was criticized a lot as a child, so now she wanted to do the right thing in her family's eyes—which to her meant staying in a job she didn't like just so that she wouldn't disappoint her parents.

I noticed that Randy really lit up when she talked about baking; her throat would just open up as she spoke, and I would hear the depth of her feelings. To open her throat up further, I suggested that she make sounds such as *la, ra,* and *ma,* and I told her to hold a blue stone in her right hand several times a day. She started using menthol on her throat and breathing the fragrance into her lungs. Sound is also very important for this area, so she started listening to beautiful music. I also encouraged her to listen to the world and to herself—and suggested that she ask herself how the world heard her. All this helped Randy to open herself up, and big changes followed. She took some baking classes, which she loved. More important, she took a leave of absence from her job to focus on creative writing for a few months; she tells me she is feeling more alive and happy than she has ever felt.

Located between and slightly above your eyebrows, the **sixth chakra**'s focus on insight, visualization, and wisdom earns it the name third eye chakra. When your third eye chakra is open, you have good intuition and imagination. If it's overactive, you may fantasize too much or even have hallucinations; if it's closed down, you might have trouble thinking for yourself and thus rely too heavily on external authorities, rigid thinking and beliefs. The natural color of the sixth chakra is indigo.

Peter was a very effective and analytical planner who said he wanted to become a little less controlled and a little more trusting. When he began having trouble finalizing his plans for a Mexican vacation he was taking with his wife, I pointed out it would be a good time for him to start following his intuition. I suggested that he bring some silver light into his third eye for three days, because silver is very soothing and softening; I also asked that he stimulate his intuitive nature with white violet and carry an amethyst crystal in his pocket. I even asked him to tape a small amethyst to his forehead when he went to bed; he laughed at me, but he did it.

A few days later, when Peter met a South American couple at his son's soccer game, he felt a sudden, strong calling to go to Brazil. He trusted the feeling, canceled his Mexico plans, and he and his wife went to Brazil. Of course they had a wonderful time. He said it was the best vacation of his life—all because he had followed his instincts. The next exercise can help you recognize your own instincts by opening your sixth chakra.

Exercise Your Spirit:	**Open Your Eye**
What you will need:	**A silver- or indigo-colored candle, salt**
Time:	**15 minutes**

- *Light a silve-r or indigo-colored candle.*
- *Sprinkle salt around you in a circle so that you are in the center of the circle.*
- *Imagine that you can breathe in and out of your sixth chakra, your third eye, and chant the following:*

My third eye can see, it is open and free.
I have strength without fear, I am open, I am clear.
From head to toes, new life in me grows.

The **seventh chakra** is the bridge to your higher self. Located at the crown of the head, the crown chakra is about wisdom and finding your place in the world. When your seventh chakra is open, you are quite aware of yourself and you view the world without prejudice. Too little activity in your crown chakra can lead to rigid thinking; too much can result in an overintellectualized outlook. The natural color of the crown chakra is purple.

My clients Sandra and Mariela came to me together looking for their shared life purpose. Sandra was raising her children, and Mariela was in the construction business, but they wanted to do more with their lives. They had lots of ideas, but without one idea that was more compelling than the others, they were simply dreamers without a dream. Once we were able to focus their energy with the Seven Keys, they created a vision of the business they wanted, something that would bring them prosperity as it enhanced and touched the lives of others. Together they founded the Aris Institute, an innovative treatment center for beauty, balance, and energy care that offers European-style treatments right here in Los Angeles. Neither of these ladies had done anything like this before, but when they were able to open their seventh chakras, they got in touch with their higher purpose. With a clear image of the future they desired, they were able to visualize the elements they needed for success.

The **eighth chakra**, or auric chakra, is the first of the five lesser-known chakras. Located in the arch on each foot, it holds the possibilities and potentials that wait for you here on earth. You must be present in your body in order to realize your potential; as the grounding point for passing energy between you and the earth, the rust-colored eighth chakra will help you manifest those possibilities by transforming body energy into earth energy (and vice versa).

When Leslie came to me, she was full of ideas for books she

wanted to write—songs and movies too. Leslie was a dreamer, but if she kept on dreaming, she was not going to get far. She couldn't focus on any single idea. I told her she needed to take one step at a time. Working with her eighth chakra enabled Leslie to settle into her body, and soon she had found a constructive way to use her talents, writing for a local newspaper. It was only a first step, but it was certainly progress—the first time she had been able to transform her thought energy into concrete results.

As the phrase "one step at a time" reminds us, we rely on our feet to move forward. Our feet take us to our real magic and move us into our higher gifts. Be good to your feet and they'll be good to you! In addition to this next exercise, try soaking your feet and then rubbing them with lotion or oil—and see how good you feel.

Exercise Your Spirit:	**Your Feet on the Ground**
What you will need:	**You**
Time:	**10 to 15 minutes**

- *Walk barefoot on the earth—sand, grass, or dirt.*
- *As you feel your feet on the earth, repeat this chant:*

> *Mother Earth, I feel you under my feet*
> *Mother Earth, I hear your heart beat*

- *Continue for ten minutes.*

The **ninth chakra**, located about three inches above the head, is the energy center of divine love, spiritual compassion, and spiritual selflessness. It also holds your karmic residue—the energy patterns that you have held on to for longer than one lifetime—as well as the possibilities released by the tenth chakra. When the ninth chakra starts to open, you begin to develop a new spiritual awareness of yourself as a part of a larger community of people and beings. Light yellow in color, the ninth chakra will open doors to many gifts when it is activated.

My client Max was a gifted and successful artist, but his success was breeding arrogance that was causing trouble in his romantic relationship. I could see his ninth chakra wasn't open, so I asked him to breathe a pale yellow light into the top of his head and spin it in a clockwise motion, making whatever sounds came to his mind as he did it. As silly as he said it made him feel, over time this exercise helped Max both develop his natural gifts even further and discover a sense of gracious humility about his life that saved his relationship.

About six inches above the crown you find the **tenth chakra—** gateway to ideas, concepts, and abilities that transcend the self, the earth, and the soul, including out-of-body projection, spiritual perception, and spiritual wisdom. Silver in color, the tenth chakra has a healing aspect so powerful that I regard it as the temple of human cleansing. When this chakra is open, you begin to get ready to shed the mundane patterns that have kept you rooted to your humanity and grasp something much larger, more wonderful, and infinitely divine. This is a natural process that removes the obstacles that keep you from uniting with higher powers, beings, and ideas.

Once this chakra is open, you have to let go of some of those outworn human ideas about yourself and the planet, which can be a shock. You may have heard that once you open the door to spirit, you are forever changed and can't go back; the opening of the tenth chakra is one of the most compelling examples of this. I've noticed that many clients who begin exploring the tenth chakra become very interested in past-life regression, for example. Clairvoyance, advanced dream recall, healing gifts, telepathy, and even empathy are other abilities that the tenth chakra activates, though you need to open the eleventh and twelfth to develop any real control over them. Because these and other experiences can be very confusing, it's important that you stay grounded so you can adjust to the new realm of possible realities rather than judge it. I advise clients who go through these changes to look at their new gifts as new forms of magic and to play with them in a very simple manner.

The **eleventh chakra** is the knowledge base of the soul, housing all the information and life experiences that are part of you, the skills and abilities learned in all your lifetimes. It sits about eight inches above the head, and its color depends on whatever skills you are pulling from its storehouse to use in the outer world. As you begin to awaken spiritually, you access this chakra to bring forth past skills that are needed in the present, merging these skills together as you synthesize all the human and spiritual lessons the soul has endured. The soul then learns the true meaning of what has been accomplished from your entire human experience, and spiritual wisdom finally sets in.

The clients with whom I've worked on opening this chakra have felt a powerful emotional release, saying that they have received knowledge that enables them to understand many of the experiences and relationships that they have had. It is as if they see their life as a puzzle and understand each piece. When you open this chakra, you will begin to manifest many of the skills you have learned in previous lives, excelling at anything you undertake as you tap into this wisdom. This chakra is responsible for divine creativity—the ability to bring all facets of your life into perfect harmony, until your life just clicks, and you seem always to be in the right place at the right time.

The **twelfth chakra** is the connection to God or Goddess, containing the path of the soul without any restrictions of matter, time, or space. When the pale golden yellow twelfth chakra is open, you will become aware that your physical reality is just one of many existences that take place on different planes of experience; you will also be in touch with the energies of self-love and acceptance, and with the peace that comes from knowing that everything is just as it should be. This expansion of consciousness can be confusing, so it's important to open this chakra in a gradual and even manner. The twelfth chakra is about a foot and a half above the head, and you can help open it by holding gentle pink light in the mind and spraying it out the top of the head like a fountain.

It's very hard to open this chakra in the city; I find that clients whose twelfth chakras are more open generally spend time outside and in the quiet of the country. Most people go through life without ever completely opening this chakra; I have seen it fully open on only a dozen people, all of whom were unusually loving. Another thing they had in common was that none of them looked their age: a seventy-year-old woman looked like she was forty, and the three-year-old child of a client seemed to have the wisdom of someone decades older. To bring yourself into this space, I think you need to be near someone else who has opened his or her twelfth chakra. If you are blessed to meet people who have activated this chakra, you will feel them as they enter your life. Listen closely and they will lead you to wholeness, fulfillment, and great spirituality. They will truly change your world.

Once you are familiar with all twelve of your chakras, you can use this technique of meditation with visualization to activate your chakras and stimulate your natural energy flow.

Exercise Your Spirit:	**Climbing the Ladder**
What you will need:	**You**
Time:	**10 minutes**

- *Sit comfortably with your spine straight and your body erect.*
- *Take a deep breath and allow yourself to be still.*
- *As you take more breaths, picture your twelve chakras spinning inside and above you like planets radiating light. (Don't forget the eighth chakra under your feet.)*
- *Picture yourself climbing into your body and using ladders to move from chakra to chakra.*
- *Move up into the light of each chakra and see yourself joining with God, Goddess, and all that is.*
- *Then see yourself sliding down through all of your chakras and ending up in your tailbone.*
- *Take another deep breath and say your name to yourself.*
- *Feel that love created you. Allow your organs to smile.*

Becoming More Sensible

In addition to twelve chakras, you also have twelve senses that you need to develop to fully use your magic. You're undoubtedly familiar with the first five—sight, hearing, touch, taste, and smell—which you use to live your life. It's important to clear away the clutter that collects in our sense system. Purifying the senses offers a way to symbolically satisfy the desire to purify one's mind and heart that is common to most of the world's spiritual traditions.

Exercise Your Spirit: **Clearing the Senses**
What you will need: **You**
Time: **Ongoing**

The sense of sight:
- *Visualize your eyes being filled with glowing light.*
- *On an ongoing basis, keep sacred images around you, and say,* Allow this beauty to grow stronger in me, *whenever you lay your eyes upon something beautiful.*

The sense of hearing:
- *Ring a bell and listen to it until it stops vibrating.*
- *On an ongoing basis, try to close your ears to unhealthy communication; if you do hear some disturbing talk or news, clear your head by ringing a bell or holding a seashell to your ears.*

The sense of taste:
- *Clear negativity from your mouth by invoking a blessing when you brush your teeth, such as,* As I cleanse my mouth, I purify my voice.

- *On an ongoing basis, chant or pray regularly to keep your speech truthful; if you accidentally say something you wish you hadn't said, rinse your mouth out with warm salt water right away.*

The sense of smell:
- *Burn some purifying incense and breathe in deeply.*
- *On an ongoing basis, whenever you smell something beautiful, say,* **What I breathe becomes me.**

The sense of touch:
- *Soak your feet and hands, focusing on the fact that such rituals of bathing are an important part of many spiritual traditions.*
- *On an ongoing basis, whenever you are in the elements, feel the power of the wind, the warmth of the sun, or the cleansing of the rain on your body.*

To combine and harmonize the first five senses, use this simple exercise to build your inner powers:

Exercise Your Spirit:	**The Ticking Clock**
What you will need:	**You**
Time:	**Ongoing**

- *Close your eyes and imagine a clock hanging on the wall, its pendulum swinging to and fro.*
- *Try to hear the clock ticking.*

- *Hold on to this double imagination of seeing and hearing for five minutes.*
- *If you begin to feel tired before five minutes have passed, stop.*
- *Practice this exercise daily for a month to strength the first five senses.*

Though we're taught as children that we have only five senses, the sixth sense, intuition, is becoming more widely recognized as a natural function that everybody has. It seems that people always want to know how to develop their intuition. The good news is that you're already doing it, simply by working with your subtle energy system—getting to know the chakras and keeping them open. This work increases your likelihood of receiving intuitive impressions in a variety of intriguing and often-unanticipated ways.

The most frequent way intuition manifests in our lives is probably through hunches, "gut" feelings, and other methods of knowing something without knowing how one knows. This sensing, or *clairsentience* (literally, "clear sensing"), is often accompanied by a physical sensation, such as a prickling of the skin or a burning in the heart. Sometimes this information comes as a thought that walks across the mind in a natural, subtle manner; in these situations, our intuition can be so much like the regular musings of our mind that we may easily miss or dismiss it or mistake it for our own ruminations.

We can also experience intuition through our primary senses: *clairvoyance*, the gift of sight; *clairaudience*, the ability to receive information through hearing, most often as a voice; and the less common *clairsavorance* and *clairscent*, which involve our senses of taste and smell, respectively. Some people have reported smelling a sudden scent—of baking cookies, perhaps, or of lilacs—at the moment of the death of a person with whom they associated that scent. Others say that they smell roses whenever they see visions of the Virgin Mary, as I do. When my client Claire asked me what it meant that she periodically smelled a particular scent in her house, I told her that she had intuitive abilities she needed to cultivate; rather than think of the scent as an omen, I suggested that she regard it as a reminder that she possessed a gift that would be everpresent. She soon became very good at smelling trouble. Claire's experience shows us that the use of this sense can protect us; trouble actually has a stink to it, as do the people who tend to thrive on it, and something or someone's "smelling fishy" can be a warning worth paying attention to. Claire uses her sense of smell to hire the right people for her company. She says she now has a high rate of stability with employees—though she has not told anyone else the secret of her hiring strategy!

Intuition can also be experienced as sensitivity to energy or vibrations. It can take such familiar forms as the ability to read minds (telepathy) or energy fields (aura perception) or to recognize angels, spirit guides, loved ones who have passed away, and other life forms from other dimensions. In addition to forms of sight, the sense of touch is involved in *psychometry,* the ability to discern information by sensing the vibration of an object held in one's hand. Insights can also come from the vibrations of a particular location or setting. My client Jason, a trial lawyer, has the gift of psychometry. The first time he came to see me, he asked to hold my watch and began to give me a reading. He was good! He just needed to hear some confirmation; once he began to trust his gift, he began to use it in his everyday life. You can probably imagine how handy that gift can be for a trial lawyer!

Sometimes the information that is received intuitively relates to a time other than the present. An individual with the gift of *precognition* is able to know about events before they occur, just as a person with the ability of *retrocognition* can know details about events from the past, such as past-life memories; these insights can come in either a conscious or a dream state and can be experienced through any of the "clear senses" discussed earlier. Nixa grew up in a devoutly Catholic family in Puerto Rico. She began to get a lot of cravings for Jewish foods and developed a keen interest in Jewish literature. We did a past life regression and found that she had many memories of being Jewish. These memories started to take over her life. When she finally surrendered to them, she actually converted and found her true love—a Jewish rabbi.

How do we distinguish intuitive information from the countless impulses we receive every day? There are a variety of ways to know when you are receiving intuitive information. Many intuitives, especially those whose strength is clairsentience, often experience physical sensations that are harbingers of truth—restlessness, discomfort, or even physical pain if the impressions are warnings, and goosebumps, tears, or warmth in the hands, spine, or heart if the insights are of a positive nature. For others, the sensations are more emotional—uneasiness or confusion, for example, or euphoria or a profound sense of peace. Sometimes it's the quality of the information itself: intuitive information often arrives with a great and unshakable sense of clarity that causes it to stand out from the rest. Pay attention to those moments of clarity; they may be your intuitive powers trying to reach you!

I always know that my inner, intuitive voice is trying to reach me when I feel it come up from my navel and move into my head. The inner voice always originates in the gut: that's why Buddha guides us to contemplate our navel. I used to get into my car and just ask to be guided to where I was most needed to be of service: I would allow my head to become a pendulum and follow its cue, and it always led me to the perfect place. The first time I did this, I drove to a bookstore, where I met a woman who had just found out she had cancer. We sat and talked for over an hour, and she told me she felt I had been sent to her. Another time my inner voice told me to stop at a house I'd never visited. Inside I met a young boy who was about to hang himself. I took him to the hospital and waited with him until his father arrived. These days people seem to be led to me, perhaps because I've continued listening to my intuitive inner voice for years. Once you are in contact with it, you never lose the connection. It takes courage to listen to it and even more courage to act upon it. You may feel silly, as I assure you I did when I found myself in front of a home I knew nothing about. My will—my core—knew something that my mind could not begin to understand and probably never will.

Though they aren't as widely discussed as intuition, the remaining six senses are just as important: balance, movement, voice, light, warmth, and substance. **Balance** involves getting different kinds of energies to work effectively together, such as male and female energies; you can strive for balance in regard to the mental, physical, spiritual, and emotional aspects of life, for example, or concerning the four elements. Without balance, one type of energy can have too much effect at the expense of other energies. One way to understand this principle is to try whenever you meet someone to determine his or her sense of overall balance. When my client Hank came to me, he was full of great ideas and constantly getting new inspirations, but he couldn't materialize any of them. Hank was very intuitive, but he was off balance, unable to get grounded enough to put his ideas to use. He had the ideas but not the ability to make them happen, and he was struggling financially as a result. We worked on his male side and his sense of himself as a man. He began to develop ideas into concrete plans and eventually found his niche as a computer programmer.

The eighth sense, **movement**, describes that subtle sensation of feeling a change before it happens. Many clients come in saying that they feel they are in the midst of a change, but they do not know what it is or when it is coming. Movement is the sense behind such situations: it allows you to feel that something is coming, the way I felt my husband moving toward me before we met. It's a hard feeling to describe—I just had this sense my life was preparing for a big change—but it's a feeling we've all had at some point. The next time you sense that something is coming your way, write it down on a calendar so you can get to know your own personal sense of timing and you can learn to trust your natural instincts.

The sense of **voice** is your ability to hear the voice of your guide or your guardian angel or your own inner voice. Many of us speak too much and listen too little; the ninth sense is a reminder of just how important listening is. One day as a client was leaving my office to head toward Laguna Beach, I heard *No! No!* loudly in my head. I gave her the message and she called the friend she was supposed to meet; sure enough, the dinner she was planning to attend had been canceled. Another client was planning to fly from Denver to Boise, Idaho, to visit her boyfriend when she heard a voice tell her not to go. She chose not to listen because she really wanted to see her boyfriend. On the drive to the airport, her taxi ran out of gas. Again she heard the voice saying not to go; this time she listened and took another taxi home. That was the Continental Airlines flight from Denver to Boise that crashed on takeoff, killing over two dozen passengers. Learning to listen to yourself might just save your life.

The **light** I speak of in the tenth sense does not mean electric light or the light of the sun. Think of the times you've met people who have a "radiant smile" or a "light" in their eyes: you were picking up on the light that they carry within themselves, just as you carry a light within you. I am sure that there are some moments when you feel your light more strongly than others, but it is always there. Meditation creates more light in the body, so much so that people can easily notice it. This little exercise can help you envision yourself as part of the world of light.

Exercise Your Spirit:	**Pure Light**
What you will need:	**You**
Time:	**10 to 15 minutes**

- *Lie down, relax, and imagine that every cell in your body can receive light.*
- *Feel your body and allow the light to expand out of it.*
- *Focus on the feeling of your body radiating light.*
- *Concentrate on the light inside your body and on how far it goes out.*
- *Let your body be porous: no skin, no edges, just exuding rays of light.*

Just as you can sense the light in people, so too can you pick up on their **warmth**. The eleventh sense is your ability to feel someone's warmth or coldness. I had a very sweet woman come in to see me who was having trouble getting pregnant. I could sense right away that she was very cold energetically, so we did some work warming up her body through the second chakra. A year later, she was introducing me to her baby boy!

The twelfth sense, **substance**, is my personal favorite. When I meet people, I always notice how they are using their soul energy. I notice that when people have substance, there is a weight to their words. They follow through with what they say. There are people who have a lot of light but have no substance. The sense of substance helps you tell whether they are really manifesting their soul. It is also an indicator for you of how well a person knows himself, how old his soul is, or how deep he is willing or able to go.

How long does it take to develop these senses? You can take as long as you want. Time is a funny thing; we can stretch it out or speed it up. Take some time over the next forty-eight hours and notice people in regard to the twelve senses. You must practice using all your senses until they become very natural to you.

Put Your Will in Your Hand

Now that you know more about your energy system, you are ready to draw on that energy to create and charge your own magic wand. My wand is a branch that I found in the Caribbean and have charged over 13,200 times. I use my wand very rarely, and only for special circumstances—to expel disease, for example, and to make big changes in clients' lives. Power is best kept hidden, so I never allow anyone to see my wand; I keep it wrapped in a beautiful silk scarf. I have named my wand, but I have never revealed its name to anyone, and I never will.

You will usually find your wand within three miles of where you live. These days this can include the Internet, but remember that your wand does not have to be something that you purchase. You might have a tree or bush in your yard that reaches its branches out to you when you pass by. Or you might find something calling to you while you're on vacation, like I did. I was in a small boat in Puerto Rico going though the mandrake trees; one branch called my name, so I turned the boat around, broke off the branch, and brought it home. One client, a very well-known actress, brought in her baton from high school! Another brought in an actual wand from her uncle's magic show in Vegas. Others have found crystal wands or have received gifts they could use as wands at just the time they were ready for one. Use your imagination and have fun with this. If you do not find your wand right away, you can still move through the exercises. Some clients who could not find their wands when they were looking for them just continued on with their studies; once they forgot about looking—bingo, their wands came to them. Or if you don't want to wait for a wand, try using a knitting needle. And remember, your real wand is the one inside you —so even if you do not find an outer wand, you will still have your magic!

Exercise Your Spirit:	**Naming Your Magic Wand**
What you will need:	**A wood or crystal wand, a silk scarf**
Time:	**1 week**

- *Once a day for a week, hold your wand next to each of your chakras, one chakra at a time.*
- *Ask your wand what its name is and listen. The name must come to you several times over a week.*
- *When you know it to be true, declare it so.*
- *Whisper the name thirteen times and wrap your wand in a clean silk scarf for forty-eight hours.*
- *Now that you have named your wand, you're ready to charge it!*

Your wand is a physical symbol or expression of your will, an extension of the same power that flows up and down your spine. Don't expect to be able to point your wand and start making things move or disappear, however. Initially you won't be able to see your results, but they'll exist first on the mental sphere, where your thoughts take place, and then on the astral sphere, where all things are created. Only later, after even more charging and practice, will your wand be able to create results on the physical level that you can see with the naked eye. The effectiveness of your wand depends on your training, maturity, and imaginative powers, as well as on what you want to create. Magical literature contends that a wand becomes powerful in the physical world usually after it has been charged 462 times. So start charging!

Exercise Your Spirit:	Charging Your Magic Wand
What you will need:	Your wand
Time:	Ongoing

- *Hold your wand in both hands.*
- *Imagine that you can bring all the energy of the universe through your body and through your hands into the wand.*
- *Concentrate your willpower into the wand with the idea that as long as the wand exists it will represent all of your will and all of your power and remain effective.*
- *Continue this for eleven minutes.*
- *Wrap the wand in silk and store it away for eleven days.*
- *Repeat the process, again for eleven minutes, increasing the intensity of the imagination and rewrapping the wand when you are finished and storing it away for another eleven days.*
- *Repeat the entire process every eleven days for as often as you like; the more often you charge it, the more power your wand will have.*

A wand charged in this way will remain effective until you die; if you charge it with the wish that it grow powerful even after your death, it may last for centuries, its influence increasing with time. It's important to keep in mind that your wand is *your* wand. Once you have charged your wand, don't let anybody else use it while you are alive. Mine has been so powerfully charged that I have left my husband clear instructions on how to use my wand after my death; he will be instructed to give it to my middle daughter, Tiffany Rose, should her will be strong enough to handle it.

Your wand embodies your entire spiritual will. Because of that, you can also use it as a battery; the energy you've stored in it is there for you to use. I use mine when I am too tired to use my will, or when I have not been feeling well. So whenever you feel fatigued, hold on to your wand and you will quickly feel yourself being recharged.

The next chapter will teach you how to use your wand with your words to create powerful magic. Your words combine your thoughts, feelings, and will; when you have aligned all three, your words can be clear, authentic, and true. With the help of your wand, you will truly make magic with your words. So be it.

CHAPTER 5

KEY **5**: Your Words Are Your Invocations

The great vowels bring radiance, and add energy when they enter; they even encourage the arms and legs to move in a certain way. The seven vowels, one could say, penetrate through the intellect to the body.

—ROBERT BLY

There is no power on this planet greater than the word. In fact, it is by the power of the word, in the word, and through the word that all things seen and unseen have been created. Remember what the Bible says: "In the beginning was the word, and the word was with God." God made use of the word to create, and so do we.

We materialize our reality through the words we use and the way we express them. Every word comes from your mouth with a color and vibration that creates or destroys your life. Our lives truly reflect our words. Our words have more power than our thoughts, so what we say will come into our lives, even more than what we think.

Whether written or spoken, our will summons the energy that brings life to our words and invokes powerful forces into our lives. An invocation is a call to a greater power, a petitioning for help or support through conjuring or incantation. We invoke with our words all the time, even more so with words that we often repeat. One way to understand the way your words take effect is to think of the way a picture taken with a Polaroid camera gradually emerges over time. The more often you repeat your words, the more results those words will create. Are you developing a picture you want to look at?

One reason words are so powerful is that they draw on more than one element. While thoughts of the mind are air and desires of the heart are water, our words can be compared to the condensation that occurs when the elements of air and water interact with each other: words are a product of both intellect and feeling, air and water. What's more, they come together as an act of will, which introduces the fire element as well. We'll also see that each word calls on one or more of all four elements, including earth. Let's bring all of the elements into our work with words with this simple exercise:

Exercise Your Spirit:	Bringing in All Elements
What you will need:	You and your wand
Time:	10 minutes

- *Make the sign of the cross from your head to your heart, then across from left to right.*
- *Hold your wand in your right hand.*
- *Close your eyes. Project your awareness and point your wand above your head and say,* I am divine.

- *Project your awareness and point your wand to the earth and say,* I am human.
- *Project your awareness and point your wand in front of you and say,* I move forward toward the light.
- *Project your awareness and point your wand to your left and say,* I see, hear and feel.
- *Open your eyes, look behind you, and, as you point your wand behind you, say,* I leave the past behind.
- *Look forward, pointing your wand, and say,* I create life with my breath.
- *After this, you may wrap your wand back up in its silk scarf and have some food and drink and say,* I celebrate life.

The mystery of the word requires the highest form of initiation. Historically, whoever mastered the word was considered the highest initiate, the highest priest, so every true magus must have command of language. To be in touch with your magic, you must learn how to appreciate and use the power of your words. If you let your heart direct your words, you will have many magical moments and begin to trust and speak from a solid place that has meaning and depth. When you talk, people will listen. When you make requests, the universe will provide. This simple exercise can get you into the habit of using your words to create the life you want.

Exercise Your Spirit:	**Make it So**
What you will need:	**You**
Time:	**A moment**

Hold your wand in your left hand and put your right hand on your second chakra (just under your belly button).

- *Think of something you want to create in your life. Feel the desire!*
- *Say what you are creating out loud.*
- *Put your wand down and clap your hands three times.*
- *Say it again.*
- *Clap your hands three times.*
- *Say it once again.*
- *Clap your hands three times.*
- *Say,* So be it!

The Beauty of Words

On the clairvoyant level, words are beautiful and magical to watch. Every letter has a color, so words come out like moving, changing color tones. The ancient mystical practice of the Kabbalah teaches us that each letter expresses an idea, and thus has its own unique powers and qualities. When you learn the principles of each letter, you can use words and letters in creative ways; before you say a word, for example, you can see the colors of its letters and put emotional energy behind each letter as it rolls out of your mouth. You actually pronounce the word with your spirit before you do so with your body.

Before going any further into these magical teachings, I want to say that I do not ascribe to any religion of the world. I feel that religion is a small fence around a great and glorious idea, an idea that I love to explore and celebrate. The teachings of the power of the word are associated with the Kabbalah, which has been traced to ancient Hebrew mysticism, but I don't speak Hebrew and you certainly don't have to speak Hebrew to understand it.

For each letter, the Kabbalah identifies a color and an element, which in turn gives you a specific feeling each time you say it. Letters that carry the element of air must be said with a feeling of ease; letters with the element of fire must be said with a feeling of warmth; letters with the element of water must be spoken with a feeling of coolness; and letters with the element of earth must be given a gravity or weight to them. When you say them, feel the different elements of the letters in different parts of your body: fire elements are felt in the head, air in the chest, water in the abdomen, and earth in the legs and feet. The element of *akasha*, which is God, is a feeling of overall power.

Magical Alphabet

A	light blue	air
B	light violet	earth
C	vermilion	fire and air (which gives feelings of ease, then warmth)
D	dark blue	fire
E	dark violet	akasha (power)
F	light green	earth
G	grass green	water
H	silver violet	fire
I	light opal	earth
J	dark opal	fire
K	silvery blue	fire
L	dark green	air
M	blue-green	water

N	red	water
O	ultramarine	earth
P	dark gray	earth
Ω	is not regarded in magical work as an individual letter.	
R	gold	fire
S	purple red	fire
Sch	blazing red	pure fire
T	brown-black	fire
U	ivory black	akasha (power)
V	is a variation of F.	
W	lilac	water
X	is not considered a letter.	
Y	pink	water
Z	lemon yellow	air

Exercise Your Spirit: **Now I Know My ABCs**
What you will need: **You**
Time: **Ongoing**

- *Stand straight or sit with a straight spine.*
- *Say the letter A to yourself, projecting its color to the space around you, imagining that its color (light blue) fills the whole room.*
- *Say the letter A inwardly still, and feel your body filling with the light blue color.*

- *Say the letter A through your mouth, and see the light blue color move around and fill the entire universe. As you do this, bring in the elemental feeling of air, which is ease.*
- *Breathe the color into your body as if your body were a hollow space.*
- *Repeat all four steps with each of the remaining letters.*

One simple, fun way to use the Kabbalah alphabet is to practice using it with your name. Each time you introduce yourself, visualize the colors that go with your name. When I do it, for instance, I see dark green (L), light blue (A), ivory black (U), gold (R), and light blue again (A). This will help you say your name with purpose and pride, building your self-esteem at the same time that you grow more familiar with the beauty and power of your words. As you practice, hold your wand with your right hand to send your name into the world with your will.

The Power of Words

I am reminded of the importance of this key every day, when I hear people sending out negative invocations. My client Claire came in recently telling me that she was "worried sick" about her daughter, who is in a relationship with a man who is very depressed. As we've seen, worry is negative prayer, so instead of trusting in her daughter's power, Claire is actually sending negative energy to someone she loves. She would be much more helpful saying, "I know my daughter will make the right decision in regard to her relationship. I am sending her love and courage to hold a space of unconditional love." But what about Claire, who is "worried sick"? If she keeps talking like that, how long do you think it is going to take her to actually get sick? I suggested to her that each time she finds herself using words that lower her and her daughter's energy, she immediately delete the message by saying aloud new words of empowerment.

Some of the most convincing evidence of the power of our words comes from people who use their words carelessly. If we use our words carelessly, other people will not listen to us, and we can inadvertently create a reality that we do not want. One young mother used to complain to me that her husband and children were driving her crazy. A few years later she had a nervous breakdown! Now she is recovering, and choosing her words with great care. These days she says her kids make her skinny, because she wants to lose weight! Clever idea: I am waiting to see how it works.

Another client came to see me full of misgivings because she had been to many other healers who could not read her energy. "I am always disappointed," she said: it was her motto. The session went well, but when she got home, she discovered that the tape we had used to record the session had malfunctioned. Once again, she had created disappointment. My client Jack kept telling me his wife was "walking herself to death," until one day his wife suffered a heart attack while walking their dog. Luckily she recovered, and Jack never uses that phrase anymore.

One of the strongest messages I have ever received about the power of our words came from a dear client named Lydia. When she was younger, her mother had died during a simple surgery, and Lydia had developed a bitter distrust of traditional western medicine. Each time we spoke, Lydia told me that western medicine was going to kill her. She also informed me, the first time I sent her a birthday card, that she didn't do birthdays: "I would not be caught dead celebrating my birthday," she said. After several years of our working together, she called one day to tell me that she had been diagnosed with breast cancer, and that she had decided she would fight it only with alternative, nonwestern treatment. I have always been deeply committed to complementary medicine, and I encouraged her to use both allopathic and alternative approaches. But Lydia wouldn't listen, and all I could do was simply love her and see her whole and healthy. I hadn't spoken to her for about six months when I found out that she had died: a minor accident had sent her to the emergency room, where in another freak accident she died. She had fulfilled her words. But there was more evidence of the power of her words still to come: as the write-up in her local paper reported, Lydia's funeral was on her birthday.

Remember how we protected ourselves against words as children? "Sticks and stones may break my bones, but words will never hurt me." Obviously they could hurt, or we wouldn't have been sending out that shield of protection! All of us, at some time in our lives, have been hurt by words. The harmful energy in words can hurt you; on a clairvoyant level, it looks like lots of little daggers flying through the air. If you're the one saying hurtful things, the little daggers go in both directions: you can hurt both yourself and the person you're talking to. That's why it's best not to say anything when someone says something hurtful to you. They're going to be on the receiving end of those daggers as well, so just let them leave their words echoing as the last words said. If you try to defend yourself, on the other hand, you're more likely to see yourself as guilty, and therefore to accept as truth whatever was said.

Often the words that hurt us the most can be our own. Whatever you say, you shall have; the subconscious carries out orders without any need of further, conscious direction. This power isn't limited to matters of life or death but can be felt in countless little ways as we go about our days. Whenever Shirley came to see me, for example, she spent the first ten minutes of her session complaining about how hard it was to find parking near my office and claiming that she would come more often if she could park more easily. I wish she could have heard what the client who came after her said: he sat down and told me how easy it was to come to my office because he always found a place to park!

Why do our words carry so much power? One reason lies in the simple fact that they can't be taken back. You can shift your mind, and change your thoughts, but once you've said or written a word, it can never be unsaid or unwritten. The vibrations that accompany each word cannot be withdrawn or erased, and it is through the vibrations that we communicate more than the words themselves. That's why if our words and meanings are not aligned, we can say or write one thing and communicate something completely different; the truth is expressed in the vibrations even if it's masked by the words. The importance of learning to use your words with care is clear: it's too easy to communicate unintended messages—to the universe, to other people, and even to ourselves.

Ana came to me because she wanted a career on the stage. She had a beautiful voice and presence about her, but she had not had any opportunities open to her. Nearing her thirtieth birthday, she was struggling financially to keep her stage career alive. I gave her this little rhyme:

Bring me riches
Bring me fame

Bring bright honor to my name
Ana
Bring it on in.

I asked Ana to repeat the rhyme to me as loud as she could and then as soft as a whisper, and this is what she said:

Bring me riches
Bring me shame

She stopped, shocked, as soon as she said "shame." We had to evaluate her feelings about money and discovered she was afraid of success. After we discussed that fear, I asked her to repeat the rhyme again. This time she whispered,

Bring me riches
Bring me pain

Again, the revealing, unexpected word seemed to come out on its own, and again we stopped to talk. I learned that Ana had grown up in a very affluent family, but her parents had divorced when she was thirteen and her father did not share his money well. She had a lot of anger about money.

Ana went to work with the Seven Keys and soon was happy to announce that she had auditioned for *Cats* and had received her first role. Since then she has worked nonstop.

Ana's experience is a reminder that we can undermine our attempts to affirm and inspire ourselves if we don't mean what we say. The rhyme I gave her can work for you too, but when you say the words you must believe them to be true.

Exercise Your Spirit:	Honor Your Name
What you will need:	**You and your magic wand**
Time:	**A moment**

- *Hold your wand in your left hand and focus your awareness on your first chakra (the tailbone).*
- *Speak these words for yourself right now, believing they are true:*

> *Bring me riches*
> *Bring me fame*
> *Bring bright honor to my name*
> *[Say your name]*
> *Bring it on in.*

- *After saying these powerful words, act as if they have already come true.*
- *Declare it: Put your wand in your right hand and stir the energy in front of each of your feet with the point of your wand and say,*

> *So be it.*
> *So it is.*

- *Repeat this exercise often to achieve success.*

If you believe in something and speak about it, you create it. If you speak of something but you don't believe in it, your words fall on deaf ears. People don't hear you. Susan said she had come to me because her husband never listened to her and she wanted to heal her relationship with him. But I noticed that her words were coated with an angry energy, and I honestly had a hard time listening to her. I couldn't imagine that it was any easier for her husband to listen either. So I gave Susan the anger exercises from Key Three to clear her heart and cleanse her words. They worked,—and soon her husband began to listen. He also began to talk to her, which is what she really wanted.

You're not getting away with anything when you say something you don't mean; curses, like chickens, come home to roost. Bob, a Hollywood producer, spent most of his first and only session with me talking about the lack of integrity of his fellow producers. He told me that he was the only one with integrity, that he couldn't trust anybody else, and that he felt that everyone was lying to him. I've learned that if people talk a lot about something, there's a good chance they don't have it, and that was certainly the case with Bob: the check he gave me bounced, then after he called and said another one was in the mail, it took two months to get to me. What would it have taken for him to say up front that he was short on cash? That is integrity.

What do you spend a lot of time talking about? What do you complain about? Are the traits you complain about in others really yours? Are you revealing more about yourself than you realize or intend? The American poet Ralph Waldo Emerson wrote, "I cannot hear your words for who you are is screaming so loudly in my ears!" If you say words that are not in sync with your thoughts and actions, your words will not be heard—but your truth will ring loud and clear nonetheless.

You Have the Power

Words can either take you to a lighter, higher vibration or take you down and wear you out. Watch your words and give them intention. When combined with your thoughts, your words are a force of tremendous power.

I learned a lot about words watching my children grow up—perhaps because children are often more connected to their magic than adults. I noticed that the intention of my children's desire often brought them the ability to create what they wanted. When my son Bo was ten years old, and we were living in Idaho, he wrote a little poem: "California is the place/That is full of my dreams/California is the place where I feel free/It is the place where I want to be." A year later we were living in California, and today he is still there as a grown man, following his dream of making movies. My oldest daughter, Natalie, asked me to create some magic words for her to become a cheerleader; she didn't get enough votes at the tryout, but two weeks later one of the girls who did win had to move with her family to another city, so my daughter got her wish. Children have strong magic when they really want something!

Most people do not pay full attention to what they say. People who know the power of the word, however, are very careful with their conversations. In my own case it took me a while to fully understand and appreciate the power of words. For example, I would often speak about "trying" and "wanting." Who wants to try all their life? Once I eliminated those words from my vocabulary, energy began to move me forward. I love Nike ads because of the simple power of their motto, "Just do it."

Now that you're more familiar with the power of the word, you're ready to learn some basic principles of how to put that power to your best use. Let's do it!

Look at the words you use and the invocations that you make.

So many of us slip into using negative words without even realizing we're doing so. Take care that your conversation isn't filled with phrases like *I am worried that, I am anxious about, I should have.* When you put out positive energy, you will receive it back.

Use your words only for blessing, healing, and prosperity. A positive tone to your words leads people to feel blessed. Gossip, on the other hand, is exhausting—both for the gossiper and the person being spoken about. Say "Bless you" as often as possible to those you meet.

Choose words that accelerate rather than words that slow you down. Words that accelerate include *I am, I love you, I am sorry, So be it,* and *amen.* Some words that slow you down are *should, maybe, try, can't, hate,* and all curse words.

Speak in the positive without any negatives. Say the end result you desire to achieve rather than what you want to avoid or get rid of; keeping the negative alive feeds the weed. Example: Say "I am working in a profession that feeds me body, mind, and soul" rather than "I am no longer working at a job I hate."

Ask for what is yours in divine grace. I would never recommend that you ask for someone's life or possessions. Example: Say "What God has given them I will receive and more!" rather than "I want John's house."

Speak in the now, rather than the future. There's no reason to put off your good. Ask for what you want in the here and now. As Ram Dass said in the title of his powerful book, "Be here now!" Example: Say "I am working in my perfect creative profession" rather than "I will be finding a job that is creative."

Use words that you really feel. You must feel it is possible when you say it; you're probably not going to attain your goal unless you believe it's within reach. Example: Say "I am earning $2,000 a week in my new business" instead of "I own a business that creates $1 million in the first week."

Include yourself in relationship to the goals you pursue. Example: Say "I am living in a new home near the ocean" instead of "I see a house near the ocean."

Be precise and concise. Use as few words as it takes to make a complete statement of what you want. Do not ramble on. Our guides and masters are busy!

Don't limit your results. Often we don't know what is possible. I had a client who wanted $3,000 a month to live on, and she created the opportunity to get a job that paid her that. She later found out that she could have had $5,000 for the job she created. The person before her was paid more!!

Exercise Your Spirit:	Create Your Dream
What you will need:	You
Time:	Ongoing

These simple steps will help you create your dream by wording it in the form of a statement that will fully draw on the power of its words.

- *Phrase it in the now, as though it is already achieved. Phrasing it as a future event seems to always keep it out of reach.*
- *Phrase it in the positive, without any negatives. Put in what you want, not what you don't want. Your*

statement should reflect the end result of what you want to achieve or manifest.

- *Include yourself in relationship to the goal.*
- *Focus on one goal per statement.*
- *Keep it simple, using as few words as possible. Choose words that have meaning to you.*
- *Be specific, but don't limit the results by including too many specifics. Leave it as open-ended as possible to allow yourself to be upgraded from what you "think" you want.*
- *End it with a word or phrase that facilitates your letting it go to a higher power, such as* **So be it, So it is, Amen,** *or the Native Americans'* **Ho.**
- *Write it down in pencil on white paper with no lines. Pencil helps to bring it to the earth, as the earth has a magnetic field and pencils contain the graphite. Writing your statement in pencil gives your statement weight.*

Use your words for healing, not hurting. This can require special attention, because sometimes the words we think we're using to heal are actually intended to do harm. Every visit, my client Jayne would ask me if I would see her husband. She really wanted him to see me and said she knew he would really learn a lot. I always said yes every time, but for months he never called. Finally she called on his behalf, and when he came to the office, he was so shut down that it was very clear that he did not want to be there at all. He had been henpecked to see me. Thank goodness, we were able to get beyond both of our expectations and ended up making the time useful. He said he had been given a lot of mixed messages about me and was really not clear why Jayne wanted him to see me. Whenever they had a disagreement, she would say, "I wish Laura could hear you now." She was using my name and my energy to build a wall between them, and he came to think of me as a drill sergeant. I called Jayne and told her I had seen her husband and that I really enjoyed meeting him. "Well, I hope it helps," she responded. "He never listens to anyone." After putting all that energy into getting him to come, she obviously never really believed it could have any positive effect. Her words were being used to hurt rather than to heal.

Trust that if your goal is in your highest interest and you stay positive and avoid doubt, it will be yours. The more you believe in your words, the more they will bring you what you want. My client Rose could give me every reason why she was never going to have another relationship and told me over and over again that she was absolutely certain it wasn't going to happen. Vibrant and beautiful at fifty-three years old, she kept saying things like "I am too old to meet anyone in Los Angeles!" and "Men in Los Angeles only want to meet younger women." Of course Rose did want a relationship, but her words and fears were getting in the way. After working with this key, she realized that she was giving mixed messages to the universe because her words and heart were out of sync. I gave Rose these words: "I attract eligible men who see my body, mind, heart, and soul." By repeating this affirmation, Rose began to use her words to create what her heart and soul really wanted. Rose is now dating a very nice man who goes against all her preconceived notions: not only is he five years younger, but she also met him right here in Los Angeles.

Use the tools of rhyming, emphasis, and repetition. Chants, prayers, and incantations have always employed these three elements of speech to draw the most power out of words. Using rhymes can be fun and can also bring about results and self-knowledge, as we did with one of the first chants we used to help us notice magic: "Clear my path/Clear my way/Help me see magic every day." Rhythm is how we change the emphasis we place on words, varying the level of force with which we say them. Just notice the difference in feeling when you say, "So be it" and "So *BE* it": you can feel the power! Repeating words and phrases can also enhance the vibration and intention of the words, especially if you return to the same place to repeat the same words. The next exercise draws on all three of these elements:

Exercise Your Spirit:	**Words to Get a New Job or Promotion**
What you will need:	**A yellow candle, musk or cinnamon oil, the key to your vehicle, your wand**
Time:	**30 minutes**

- *Use the key to your vehicle to carve in a yellow candle your name and the name of the position you wish to obtain.*
- *Rub the candle with oil, such as musk or cinnamon.*

- *Place the candle in a candleholder, light it, and visualize your phone ringing.*
- *Imagine your excitement at getting the news that you've gotten the job you desire, calling your family and friends to share the news, hearing everyone calling you by the position title you want.*
- *After the candle has burned at least halfway, extinguish it.*
- *Pick up your wand with your right hand and stir the energy in front of your feet.*
- *Say* So be it *three times as follows:*

So be it.

So BE it.

So BEING it.

- *The next day, light the candle again and do the same visualization.*
- *Let the candle burn all the way down.*
- *Say* So be it *three times as follows:*

So be it.

So BE it.

So BEING it.

- *If there's any wax left over, bury it within a block of the building in which you would like to work.*
- *Repeat three times holding your wand in your right hand:*

New work comes to me

Bring its creativity for all to see

Move me forward into life
Take away my fear and strife.

Pay attention to the spaces between words. When people get quiet, the golden energy of the heart begins to flow through their bodies and out of their hands. But some people never stay quiet long enough for this to happen. I've told many of my clients that they just talk too much: they give people more than they can receive. It's useful to think of a conversation as a meal, with an hors d'oeuvre, salad, main course, and dessert. Instead of rushing through, you want to take a break between each course and save room for what's next. Leave time to digest what you're saying and hearing.

Notice the effect people have on you. Do they leave you feeling energized or exhausted? Their words play a big role in this—just as yours play a role in the effect you have on others. I recently spent the weekend with a friend I hadn't seen in a while, who brought her sister Charlotte along. Charlotte just talked nonstop, from one story to another, and I quickly grew very tired. She was unable, however, to see the effect of her words on me or on the world around her. When she called to make dinner reservations, she was put on hold for a long time and ultimately was disconnected; I went to the phone, called the restaurant, and made the reservation. I noticed that whenever Charlotte asked someone for something, people didn't hear her or didn't listen, even waiters: when she ordered her food, it was delivered late and wrong. Charlotte was careless with her words, too busy talking to listen, and her life reflected her carelessness.

Tell the truth. Lying is a form of covering pain with words that do not matter. Instead of conveying the truth, the words of our lies are asking for help. They are a product of our fear—fear that we do not need to hold on to. Once we let go of the fear and the pain that is behind our lies we can tell the truth.

Jackson, who had alcoholic parents, learned to lie at an early age: he needed to survive. It was not until his late twenties, when we went through the Seven Keys, that Jackson learned he did not have to live in shame any longer. Once he worked with Key Three to forgive himself, Jackson began to understand the power of his words. He saw that he did not have to make things up to be safe or to be loved or to keep trouble away; he could speak his truth, opinion, and experience without pain or hesitation.

We hurt ourselves when we allow fear to control our words. Another client of mine, Theresa, used to lie about lots of little, unimportant things. She admitted to me that she did this because she didn't feel that her life was significant enough. But until she told the truth, I found it hard to listen to her; I would begin to get very tired, and my eyes wanted to close. As soon as she admitted the truth and talked about her lying, however, her words began to actually take shape and have illumination. Once she brought her lying to the light, it was very difficult for her to lie anymore; lying began to physically hurt her body, and she stopped. She began to listen to herself, and others began to listen to her.

Keep your word. There was a day when a person was only as good as his word, but the time-honored, sacred bond of giving our word is fast becoming a thing of the past. Keeping your word is not a gray issue: when you say you're going to make something happen, you either make it happen or you don't. If you fail to produce the result that you said you would, then no number of reasons, excuses, justifications, or apologies can alter that fact. Reasons are one thing; results are something completely different.

The Law of Energy tells us that we are all connected and live in the same society, so keeping our word has consequences for all of us. As you honor the law of karma, it is in your best interests to become known as someone who can be depended on to keep your word, rather than someone who knows all the reasons why you don't.

Bianca came to her first appointment thirty minutes late. She told me she had been stuck in traffic. She obviously expected a full hour, but at the end of thirty minutes I handed her the tape of our session and sent her on her way. She called from her car with "just one more question." Becasue of my schedule, I did not return her call until the end of the day, and when I got her on the phone, she was very upset that she had received only thirty minutes of my time after paying for an hour. Six months later she made another hour appointment, and this time she arrived forty-five minutes late, explaining that her mother had borrowed her car. She had an excuse for everything, but excuses were not enough. She had made two time commitments that she had not respected. I was looking for her to keep her word and told her so. It seems that Bianca had been getting away with this behavior for a long time and no one had said, "No!" I told her she would have to give me her word that she would be there on time if she wanted to make another appointment with me. She arrived ten minutes early and has never ever made me wait again.

How good is your word? When you give your word, look some-one in the eye, make a promise, and seal it with a handshake, and then have the strength of character to honor it. Your word will then be solid gold.

Write with care and intention. As long as people have been writing, they've been writing spells. A spell is really just an organized prayer. The Sumerians are believed to have developed the first primitive alphabet in southern Mesopotamia about 3100 BC, and some of their clay tablets featured inscriptions that seem to be prayers or spells; most experts agree that the ancient Egyptians produced the most extensive collections of written spells in human history. When you write an affirmation, the act of writing imbues your words with extra power by enabling you to focus on your wish and create energy to attract it to you.

Clients often ask me if it matters when they do their writing; I tell them to choose a time of day to write words based on what kinds of words they're writing. Mornings are the best time to do things that have to do with new beginnings—a new job, home, or romance, for example. Noon, the solar hour that deals with health and energy, is good for increasing things—such as expanding a business or adding passion to a love affair. Twilight is the best time for spirituality, emotions, or contacting the spirit realm; it's also a good time to end things or to stop habits. Midnight is the time to write secrets. Also, anything said at midnight has special power, so if you're not sure when to write a wish, write it at midnight.

Exercise Your Spirit:	**Writing Your Wish**
What you will need:	**A pencil and paper**
	that contains cotton
Time:	**As long as you wish**

- *Choose a special pencil that you use only for affirmations. Don't let anybody else touch this pencil, as you are using it in effect to write letters to the divine spirit. The graphite in the pencil will utilize the gravity of the earth to bring your wishes to completion.*
- *Begin writing when you have some time in which you are sure you will not be disturbed.*
- *Write your wish with pencil in longhand; your powers of concentration are most natural when you are using your natural writing style.*
- *Allow the energy to flow from your heart into your hand. The energy then streams from your pencil and takes form on the paper.*
- *Keep your language as simple and straightforward as possible.*
- *Finish your statement of your wish by writing the sentence,* So be it.
- *When you have finished writing, fold the paper and place it somewhere that you won't see it and no one else will find it.*
- *Do not tell anybody about your wish.*
- *Keep the paper until the goal has been achieved.*

Use other tools to give your words more power. Oils, candles, and rituals can help draw out and magnify the power of your words in ways that are surprising and profound. The scents and herbs in the next exercise make the chant at its conclusion all the more effective.

Exercise Your Spirit:	**Honoring the Spirit**
What you will need:	**2 or 3 sprigs of rosemary**
	3 cups of water
	A jar of honey
	One gold taper candle
	3 sticks of frankincense incense
	Matches
	½ cup of milk
	One small bottle of any floral oil that you love
Time:	**30–40 minutes**

- *Simmer the rosemary in the water for about twenty minutes, then bring it and all your supplies into your bathroom.*
- *Rub honey all over your face, neck, and chest.*
- *Rinse your hands and dry them as you run a hot bath.*
- *Pour half the rosemary water into the bath.*
- *Light the candle and incense and sink into the water.*
- *Close your eyes and spend twenty minutes meditating or contemplating the beauty of your soul.*
- *Rinse off the honey and splash the milk on your face.*
- *Close your eyes and let the beauty of your soul ooze out of your pores as if it could boil the milk.*

- *Rinse off and pour the remaining rosemary water over yourself as a final wash.*
- *Pat your skin dry and take time to apply the oil to your skin.*
- *Chant seven times,* **Grace is with me. Peace is with me. Let beauty shine from within my soul on all I meet. So be it.**
- *Repeat this ritual three nights in a row.*

Words That Heal

When you use your words with care, the quality of your mental vibration changes for the better, enabling you to elevate others and heal the planet. You can also heal yourself: our words can help release us from pain—mental, emotional, spiritual, or physical. Pain is a creation of the mind that takes hold when we believe that we're victims, that we have no choice but to feel pain. The more pain we expect, the more we usually feel. But we can release ourselves from pain by saying these words with force:

I chose this life
I choose this life
I choose this body
I choose this pain.
I choose freedom
I choose this place, this time, this day
To make this pain go away.

Sometimes it's necessary to yell these words. Don't hold back! Remember, you are not a victim if you don't believe yourself to be one. After repeating these words, you will feel your pain begin to dissolve. I discovered this myself when experiencing terrible physical pain. One day I acknowledged that I had chosen it, and it began to dissolve and my body softened. Many of my clients have experienced great relief over time using those magic words. If you create it, then you can take it away!

Words That Uplift

Blessings are one of the most remarkable and powerful ways to uplift humanity. You can bless anything or anyone. Words of blessing carry qualities of love, peace, and light that bring us closer to perfect attunement with the invisible higher powers, surrounding others and ourselves with nurturing, protective vibrations. When we are speaking words of blessing, our chakras naturally seem to move into harmony and open up. As soon as you quiet your mind and attune yourself to your higher power, the energy in your body follows and uplifts you.

You may already be saying blessings with food, for example. Many of us are accustomed to regularly saying a blessing before we eat. This is a good idea because food is handled by lots of different people on its way to you; if you eat food that isn't blessed, you are at the mercy of the vibrations of those other people. When food is blessed, its vibrations are raised to a higher level; you transform it to love before it enters your body. If you bless yourself and those around you, you are in a state of grace when you eat, and the food will enhance what is highest in you. Eating will be a positive experience, nourishing body and soul and simultaneously conferring a grace upon what is eaten.

To add magic to your meal, visualize a circle of light around your table and ask that the food help you accomplish a goal. If you want to meet someone, for example, ask that the food goes into your body and creates a magnetism to bring your true love to you. Or if you need healing, close your eyes and ask that the food be a healing force to your body, mind, and spirit.

In addition to blessings, I often repeat mantras that teachers have given me at many stages of my journey. A *mantra* is a phrase or sentence that gains transformative power as it is repeated. The consistent practice of chanting or listening to mantras can bring a variety of important benefits and move you from negativity to positivity, from darkness to light. This mantra, given to me by Gail Rich, a magical woman in Australia, draws on the power of Latin, which is a mother tongue.

Exercise Your Spirit: **Clear Words**
What you will need: **You**
Time: **Ongoing**

Repeat these words 7 times in the morning and evening, and feel the Latin words move into your spirit:

Claria, Vitalia, Crystallia
I am clear, I am vital, I am strong
I am beautiful
Every day in every way I get better and better
Every day in every way
I am at peace with myself and the world
that surrounds me

I am in tune with the universe and the infinite
I am light
I am love

I received the next mantra from a dear friend, a Universal Kabbalistic teacher named Joseph Michael Levry. I call it the light trap, because once you start using it, you cannot stop! It works on many levels—mental, spiritual, emotional, and physical—and I've seen it replace fear, insecurity, and doubt with the peaceful stillness from which love, creativity, intuitive sight, and conscious clarity can emerge.

The mantra contains eight sounds that are repeated over and over: *Ra Ma Da Sa Sa Say So Hung.* When said once for each year of your life, the mantra can purify your energy field, which assists in self-healing; a consistent chanting practice can have a profound, positive impact on both the conscious and subconscious mind, boosting self-confidence and nurturing your deepest intuitional conviction. In moments of anxiety, despair, fear, or worry, let it be your safeguard; it will give you a strong sense of your own centeredness. Joseph Levy has many beautiful mantras in CD form available at rootlight.com.

As you chant this mantra, you expand toward the infinite and merge back with the finite. Most people have forgotten that their essence is with the infinite, unlimited creative power of the cosmos. When you go within yourself and consciously experience your own beauty, you touch your divinity directly.

This mantra is a pure divine thought. When you think pure thoughts and are mentally strong, you can better deal with the painful effects of bad karma or disease. When you regularly pray and meditate, you go into the land of light, where all troubles disappear.

Chanting in the early hours, before the sun has risen, will connect you with the cosmic energy at the time of day when the channels to the divine are the most clear. It's also especially good to practice chanting meditation at sunset, or whenever the sun forms a sixty-degree angle to you. Try chanting or praying as you meditate on the light of the sun. See if you can build up to doing this for one minute for each year of your life. Consider setting a goal of making this a daily practice; the more often you do it, the more likely you'll be to overcome your challenges and rule your destiny. In the words of Yogi Bhajan, master of White Tantric and Kundalini Yoga, who openly taught this healing mantra to the western world, "It has worked for three thousand, four thousand years, why should it not work now?"

End Your Day with a Smile

One of the secrets to a magical life is to learn to count your blessings every day. Your life is filled with blessings that you may not recognize; they can be as all-important as a loved one and a healthy body and as tiny and fleeting as a smile you received. This is how you count them at bedtime to go to sleep with gratitude in your heart and a smile on your lips.

Exercise Your Spirit:	Count Your Blessings
What you will need:	You
Time:	5 minutes

- *Before you go to bed, spend five minutes analyzing the blessings you have right now.*
- *Say your thanks for each blessing, as you think of it, out loud. (For example,* Thank you for my home, Thank you for my health.)
- *When you are finished, say,* May blessings multiply for all.
- *Ask your organs to smile as you fall asleep.*

It is time to nurture your spirit and illuminate your life. The next chapter will show you simple and practical ways of working with your angels and asking the universe for what you want. You will begin to experience how loved you truly are.

CHAPTER 6

KEY **6:** You Must Ask in Order to Receive

*The angels if they deem to come do so not because of your tears;
But because of your constant resolve to be a beginner.*

—GOETHE

When was the last time you tried to contact your angels—or your angels tried to contact you? We live in a wonderfully interactive universe. Everywhere we go, we are surrounded by helpers that we cannot see: guides, spirits of people who have passed away, and most especially angels. Angels are with us all the time, watching over us as they gently guide us to our magic. They love to help us and enjoy doing more, but they can't intervene on their own. If you want extra help from your angels, you must ask for it!

When you connect with the universe's messengers of grace, you can align with your purpose and tap into your magic. You may have been diverted from the experience of grace by old fears and inhibiting beliefs, but the universe is eager to help you restore it. You just have to know whom—and how—to ask.

Mandy walks into my office surrounded by ten angels. I ask them why she has so many, and they answer, "Because she slips through our fingers!" Mandy laughs when I tell her this, because she knows it's true: with her strong personality, she has a hard time staying out of trouble!

Connie has a difficult decision to make: she's been offered a promotion that requires a move to London, but she's not sure she wants to move overseas. Connie recognizes that in the banking industry in which she works, she may sabotage her career if she turns down the job, so she requests a sign from the universe, asking to see a ladybug in three days' time if she is supposed to accept the offer. On the third day, a dog she's never seen before shows up at her door. The name on its tag? Ladybug! Connie takes the job and moves to London, and her career takes off.

During one of my meditation/prayer services, Alison sees herself beside a river and looks across and sees an angel with two children on the opposite bank. Though she is not involved with anyone at the time, Alison feels the angel is her husband-to-be. Six months later she meets a wonderful widower with two children; they marry and she loves the children as her very own.

Do you believe in angels? Most of us do—more than two-thirds of us, according to a survey conducted by *Time* magazine (12/27/93). And almost half of those surveyed believe in guardian angels. In other words, you're not alone in believing that you're not alone! I'm going to introduce you to your helpers and show you some fun ways to ask for what you want. You'll also learn how to request and receive signs and other assistance from the universe. And as you explore the use of candles and stones and create your own personal talisman, you'll discover more sets of tools to help you make your dreams come true.

An angel is a pure spirit created by God, Goddess, All That Is. The English word *angel comes from the Greek* angelos, which means "messenger." The Bible almost always depicts angels as heavenly beings, but the term can also apply to human messengers. There is no doubt that even these human messengers are on heavenly missions: they are sent by God/Goddess for the benefit of us all.

I have never seen a person who doesn't have any angels around him or her, though a lot of people don't acknowledge or communicate with their angels. It's up to us to try to communicate: the angels tell me they cannot intercede in our lives unless we ask. A lot of us don't ask, or don't ask for enough. Some people just use their angels to find parking places. They don't realize what they're missing!

You probably already know at least a little about angels, but if you're going to try to contact them, it's worth it to find out more. Because of my connection to the Madonna, who is queen of the angels, I am often in contact with angels and have been learning a lot about them. Angels are divided into three tiers of three choirs each. The first tier includes the thrones, the cherubim, and the seraphim. The Thrones are closest to the source of divine light; they're the ones to pray to when you pray for world peace. The seraphim are all about divine love; they appear as electrical outlines of light and always travel in groups of three. The word *cherubim* means "fullness of knowledge," and they possess extraordinary wisdom, carrying the divine science of heaven. Both the seraphim and cherubim are mostly involved with bringing light to the lesser choirs of angels.

The angels of the second tier—the dominations, the virtues, and the powers—are more concerned with the management of human affairs. But it's the angels of the third tier that are most directly involved in the visible world of man: the principalities, the archangels, and the angels. The principalities guard the nations of the earth. The most important missions of man are entrusted to the archangels, who watch over the world and bring messages to people. Sometimes the archangels also serve as guardians to people who have special work to do on earth. But for the rest of us, our guardian angels come from the ranks of the other third-tier angels, the ordinary messengers sent to be protective and loving to everyone.

The four main archangels are the angels I work with the most. Michael and Gabriel are the only two archangels mentioned by name in the Old Testament; the other two are Raphael, who is mentioned in Catholic texts, and Uriel, who is discussed in the Book of Tobias. Each of them is partnered with a female angel as well; I started encountering the female archangels doing prayer and mediation workshops and ceremonies, but they are less well known than their male counterparts.

Whenever I encounter an archangel, I can feel a powerful presence. Suddenly the room I'm in turns very cold, and then my hands feel like I've put them in an icy mountain stream. The archangels have a metallic shine to their energy, and they have the ability to get very, very large, as big as the sky. What's most striking about them is their eyes: they have the most beautiful dark blue eyes, which they can use to shine light into your very soul. Archangels watch over the whole world, but they can also respond to your specific requests for help. Since each Archangel has its own angelic dominion, it's important to know about their individual characteristics.

The archangel **Michael** ranks as the highest of the host; he is considered foremost among all the angels by all three of the world's major monotheistic religions. Roughly translated, his name means "who is as God," and his position is closest to the source. Heaven's greatest defender and mightiest warrior against evil, he is usually depicted wearing armor and carrying a fiery sword, which is often used as his symbol.

When we call for his assistance, Michael protects our consciousness, our being, and our world. The angel presiding over the best parts of humanity as well as over chaos, he is the archangel to whom we turn to strengthen our faith, free ourselves from doubt and fear, inspire our leaders, and safeguard our governments. Michael is associated with the fire element, so he is helpful in matters of the will. His female counterpart is Faith, who is a bright blue angel. They are both at their strongest during the fall equinox.

The Archangel **Gabriel** is usually considered a more benevolent spirit than Michael. He is most often noted as the angel who visited the Virgin Mary to tell her of the impending birth of Christ. The word *Gabriel* can be translated as both "God is my strength" and "hero of God," and he is characteristically shown sitting at the left hand of God, majestically outfitted with crown and scepter.

Gabriel is the angel who selects the heavenly souls to be born on earth and spends the next nine months informing the child of what he or she will need to know on earth. According to legend, Gabriel silences each child before birth by pressing his finger onto the child's lips, thereby producing the cleft beneath the nose. The angel of incarnation, conception, and birth, Gabriel has helped many of my clients get pregnant when they were having difficulty. Known as the angel who watches over paradise, he is the archangel to ask for guidance in your spiritual life and for clarity in your life purpose, as well as fulfillment, encouragement, and the bringing of discipline and order to your life. Gabriel is associated with the water element, so he is especially helpful when feelings and emotions are involved. His counterpart is Hope, who is the purest white light I have ever seen. They are both very accessible during the winter solstice.

The archangel **Raphael** is the patron of the sciences and medicine, the angel over the spirits of men. His name can be translated as either "God has healed" or "the medicine of God." Granted the gift of healing by God, Raphael protects travelers and heals the sick and injured. He is the angel to whom we appeal for healing of body, mind, heart, and soul. Associated with the air element, the element of the mind, Raphael can be a source of divine inspiration for the study and practice of science, medicine, mathematics, and music. Raphael can also help you meet your material needs, such as food, clothing, shelter, and tools of your trade. Call him in for healing of the physical, emotional, mental, or spiritual. His female counterpart is Charity, who always appears in bright green. They are both with us during the spring equinox.

Also known as Auriel, the archangel **Uriel** is the angel over the world, the angel most closely associated with the earth element. His name means "fire of God," and he is often depicted holding a flame in his open hand. Uriel is the angel of music, poetry, and prophecy. We appeal to Uriel for help communicating and for dealing with material and earthly matters; we can also turn to Uriel for forgiveness. Uriel is the "initiator" to those on a spiritual journey. I have seen him alongside those who are starting their self-discovery. His counterpart is Grace, who is ruby and gold. They join us during the summer solstice.

When you call upon the archangels, it's best to pray for the benefit of others rather than for yourself. In difficult situations, however, you can ask for help. To do so, review the angels' characteristics to see which is the most appropriate archangel for your specific situation. After you've decided which angel can best help you, write your request on a plain piece of paper as follows:

> **_Dear Angel of my heart_** [write the angel's name]
> **_Help me to accomplish_** [write your request]
> **_Thank you_**

Fold up the paper and keep it with you during the day.

When my client Larry's brother had been sent to the war in Iraq, Larry came to me in tears, terrified that his brother was going to die. I asked him to write a note to the archangel Michael using really fine parchment. I also suggested that he burn a red candle for Michael and a blue candle for peace, allowing them to burn out on their own in a safe place. Larry said that as soon as he lit the candles, he felt a very strong presence in the room—so strong that he was surprised that he didn't actually see an angel in armor when he looked up. Larry's brother did serve in Iraq but ended up being discharged because of a problem with his eyes—a problem that cleared up very quickly once he got home.

Whenever you call on any angel, you need first to enhance your light body. The higher spheres are cold, so when you are working with angels, expect the room temperature to drop. Clients even get cold when we're doing phone sessions and we're not in the same room. We'll be in different states, on the phone, all wrapped up in blankets on a hot day!

Exercise Your Spirit:	Prepare to Reach Your Angels
What you will need:	You
Time:	15 minutes

- *Inhale through the mouth, bringing the breath into the solar plexus (third chakra).*
- *Close your lips and exhale through the nose, feeling the breath bringing light from the heart center (fourth chakra).*
- *Continue to inhale fire, exhale light for about ten minutes.*

You can call on just one angel, or you can call four archangels at the same time, which I always do for ceremony with the following ritual. The most important part of this invocation is visualizing the angels in your mind's eye. This is where your mental training and imagination can really make a difference!

Exercise Your Spirit:	Calling Archangels
What you will need:	Four candles, your magic wand
Time:	15 to 20 minutes

- *Light four candles, one for each archangel.*
- *Extend your arms in the form of a cross. With your wand in your right hand, say:*

     Come before me, Raphael (Rah-fay-el).

- *In your mind's eye, see Raphael coming from the east, the archangel of air holding a wand as he towers over you, his yellow robes blowing in the wind.*
- *Move your wand to your left hand and say:*

     Stand behind me, Gabriel (Gab-ray-el).

- *In your mind's eye, see the archangel of water holding a cup from which water flows; as he comes from the west, his robe is shimmering blue with overtones of orange.*
- *Move your wand back to your right hand and say:*

     On my right side, Michael (Mee-kay-el).

- *See the archangel of fire approach from the south, holding a sword and clothed in robes of flashing red.*
- *Move your wand back to your left hand and say:*

     On my left side, Auriel (Or-ray-el).

- *From the north, see the archangel of earth clothed in rich colors of the seasons—citrine, olive, russet, and black—as he stands on a disk of gold.*

Once you have called in the archangels, there's no need to try to dismiss them: these powerful, majestic spirits will come and go as they please. Just stay open to your feelings and listen to what happens when you call them in. As you proceed with your request, meditation, or ceremony, you will feel the room cool down and other unusual things may happen. You may feel a tingling sensation on your body or just an awareness of a shift in the energy of the room. Jimmy called in Raphael to help him heal his cancer. He says he felt the cold energy and then a heat went through his body. Soon afterward, he found a doctor who was doing new research on his type of cancer, and now he is on a healing path.

Queen of the Angels

As the queen of the angels, Mother Mary is prayed to by more people than any other angel. All over the world, people pray to the Mother each day. Mary has often told me how much she loves to hear these prayers, and over the years that we have been communicating, she has taught me different ways to pray to her. One of the prayers she gave me touches on the importance of saving the children of the world, the theme of many of her messages:

> *Oh Mary, you show us the way,*
> *Oh Mary, you show us the way to pray.*
> *Can I feel your feet beside me*
> *body, mind, and soul*
> *Help us now to teach the children*
> *what they need to know.*

Among the prayers she hears the most often is the rosary, or the "Hail Mary." One well-said Hail Mary fills the heart of Our Mother with delight and brings more graces to whoever says it than a great many more prayers said quickly. She has also given me a version of the rosary that she called the "mystic rosary," which is slightly different from the prayer familiar to the Catholics of the world:

Hail Mary, full of grace;
the Lord is with thee:
Blessed art thou amongst men and women,
and blessed is the fruit of thy womb, Jesus.
Holy Mary, Mother of God,
Pray for us now
and at this hour of our lives. Amen.

When we know its value and understand its beauties, the rosary is like a mine of gold that we can always take from but never exhaust. To those who recite the rosary, the Mother promises many gifts: the flourishing of virtue and good works; special protection; the destruction of vices; and the reward of all that we ask of her. As children run to their mothers for help when they are in trouble, so ought we to run with unbounded confidence to Mary.

The rosary is most powerful when it is recited as you hold a strand of rosary beads, which are widely available in many beautiful varieties. When shopping for rosary beads, just be on the lookout for the beads that resonate with you. Stones will speak to you if you're willing and ready to listen! The stories of clients who use this mystic rosary that I was given are truly heartwarming, from women who have been trying to have a baby to men who could not find work. It is the most powerful prayer that I have ever used, and I find that it brings about results without fail. One client, Robert, was tormented because he had fallen in love with a woman who he felt would never feel the same about him. I asked him to pray the mystic rosary, and although he was Methodist, he purchased a strand of rosary beads and began. He shared his feelings with this woman and now they are together and are starting a family. Another client began doing the mystic rosary as he underwent treatment for bone cancer; he prayed the rosary without fail each day, and his cancer has since gone into remission.

We can add more power to our prayers by the way we use our hands and fingers. Each finger has its own meaning and its own best position in prayer. The thumb is symbolic of our humanness; it is good to hold the thumbs together when asking for forgiveness. The index finger is the finger of the mind; putting your thumb and index finger together can strengthen your focus. The middle finger is the finger of spirit; hold your two middle fingers together when you ask for spiritual guidance. The ring finger is love, so holding it together with the thumb will bring love to your human form. Finally, the little finger represents earth; I use it with the thumb to ask for financial assistance or to meet the correct people.

Angels Everywhere

In addition to Mary and the archangels, we are all watched over by our guardian angels. Each of us has a personal team of guardian angels that come with us at birth to protect us and guide us to our true purpose. Guardian angels are always coming into my office with my clients, often with messages for me to pass on to them. They are there for us to call upon at any time to get answers for ourselves. You probably already do this more than you realize. Think of all the hunches, visions, and ideas you get every day. Now imagine how life would be if you tapped into this tremendous wisdom all the time!

The next exercises draw on your powers of visualization to help you get in touch with the angel within you.

Exercise Your Spirit:	**You Are An Angel**
What you will need:	**A mirror**
Time:	**A moment**

- *Look in the mirror and say,*

> *You are an angel*
> *It is so plain to see*
> *You are an angel*
> *Yes, the angel is me!*

You *are* an angel—yes, each and every one of you. Why would you just want to believe in angels when you can be one? It is time to own that angelic energy and find your wings!

Exercise Your Spirit:	**Spread Your Wings**
What you will need:	**You**
Time:	**12 minutes**

- *Sit quietly and breathe deeply and slowly.*
- *Imagine that between your shoulder blades is a space that holds your own angel wings.*

- *As you breathe, allow the wings to unfold and come out.*
- *Notice the size and color of the wings.*
- *With each new breath, let the wings become fuller, expanding them further out to cover someone you love, then your house, then your city, your state, your nation, and the world.*
- *Keep your wings out the rest of the day and each and every day!*

The angels' loving presence can provide uplift, relief from pain and grief, and evidence that life continues after death. They are perhaps the most vivid reminders that we live in an interactive world, and their message that we are not alone can take many forms and evoke a variety of feelings and reactions.

Often I've seen angels bring comfort to people saddened by loss. I had the honor of sitting at the bedside of Noel, a six-year-old with leukemia, who was in the final stages of her life. Noel drew me a lot of pictures and they always had angels in them. She told me that she knew she was going to live with angels and said that she hoped I would help her mommy believe in angels as much as she did. Not long after Noel's funeral, her mother called to tell me about all the angels she was seeing. One angel had appeared in the snow in front of her house in the exact place that Noel had built her first and only snowman. And every day, the mail brought more cards, letters, and packages with angels on them. Messages were everywhere, and they just kept coming. She believed!

When I was working with the dying, I often saw angels giving comfort to the men and women who were leaving. I once sat at the bed of an older gentleman who was telling me how he met his wife, who had died years before; before he could finish, his angel appeared and told me the rest of the story! I stopped the gentleman, repeated what the angel had told me, and asked if I had heard the right thing. His face just lit up with the biggest grin. When I told him his angel was nearby, he asked if he could speak to his wife. I could see his wife but I could not hear her voice, so we communicated through his angel. Shortly before he died, he told me that he had seen a doctor he didn't recognize standing silently by his bed. The man he described sounded very much like the angel I had seen. We asked if a new doctor had been assigned to his case and were told no. To this day I feel his angel paid him a visit. He died beautifully—full of peace.

Some of the most wonderful comfort that the angels bring involves messages of life after death. Over the years many clients have shared stories of departed loved ones reaching out to them, and I've seen it happen in my life as well. Linda, one of my dearest friends, came to me because her sister Roberta was in the final stages of cancer; always looking for some way to help her sister, Linda flew Roberta in from Chicago to come meet with me. Roberta was one of those people who change your world forever—her energy was so positive and her faith so strong, despite her body's inability to stay with us. She believed in angels and told her family that she would send them a message after her passing.

About a year after Roberta died, Linda went to a medium, who talked about buying blue roses at a small village in Italy. Linda had taken Roberta to the same village! Afterward Linda asked me if I had ever seen a blue rose. Of course, from then on we began to see them everywhere. Linda had put together a CD of Roberta's favorite music to give to people who loved her, and the day after the show Linda went to pick up the cover the designer had created for the CD. There on the cover was a blue rose! Our lives are now constantly filled with blue roses—little reminders from Roberta that she is still with us.

Whenever I am asked to communicate with loved ones who have passed on, I am grateful my gifts can bring peace to my clients. Such contact can resolve unfinished communication and provide evidence that death does not stop our loved ones from watching over us. We can call on our angels for help reaching out to the spirit world, and the following exercise shows you how. Keep in mind that it's best to wait six months to contact anyone who suffered greatly before they passed, though sometimes this communication can happen naturally and spontaneously on its own.

Exercise Your Spirit:	Contacting the Spirit World
What you will need:	A photo of your loved one, a white candle, your magic notebook
Time:	30 to 45 minutes

- *Place a photo of the person you wish to speak to in front of you.*
- *Light a white candle.*
- *Ask your angels to give you permission to speak to the spirit world. Ask to speak to the person who has passed on.*

- *Listen to what you hear, and write it down in your notebook.*
- *Say anything to them that you wish and be sure to pay attention to what you hear in your inner voice and see on the screen of your mind.*
- *Trust whatever you hear and see. Sometimes it is symbolic.*
- *When you are finished, always thank your angels for their time and their love.*

Angels have lots of ways of letting us know that they are around. They love bright and shiny objects and will often leave a certain coin to let you know that they're nearby. Maybe that's where the phrase "pennies from heaven" comes from—although nowadays I think they prefer dimes! They like to leave dimes behind as messages, so whenever you find one, take note of what you were thinking or talking about just before you found it. I first noticed this when I was at a fountain and noticed all the cherubim playing in the water: they were attracted to the coins. Soon after, I heard many clients tell me stories about finding dimes at special times in their lives. Angels enjoy blinking streetlights at us and playing with lights in our homes, so take note of whenever that happens too!

Angels also love music and children; put these two things together and you'll have a room full of happy angels! I cannot stop crying whenever I see a children's choir because of all the angels I see in the room. To watch a group of angels at work or play is a truly wonderful sight, and when they start to dance to the music, they make a symphony of colors. Their bodies are luminous and shiny, and they float through the air with delicate grace.

Sometimes angels can also show up in what appears to be

human form. One night I took my client Marla to the beach in Malibu to do a ritual to call in her true love. As part of the ritual, she needed to gather enough bits of driftwood or paper from the beach to build a small fire. She was having a hard time finding anything until a young woman showed up, handed her some bark, and smiled. Marla looked at me and we laughed in delight. Later in the ritual Marla was supposed to go into the water, or at least put her feet in, but she claimed it was too cold to get wet. At this point a beautiful young man appeared. "It is an amazing night," he said. "The water is warmer than the air." He walked away and disappeared into the water. That was all Marla had to hear; she completed the ritual of love and we drove home. Within two months she had met the man to whom she is now happily married. The angels wanted them to be together.

I have also seen and heard of angel's taking animal form. One night my client Sylvia fell asleep in the bathtub with a candle burning; her cat woke her up just as the candle was going to set fire to the towel—one of many times she says her cat has protected her. Once when I was moving, the packers accidentally packed up my son's medication. I looked at all the boxes piled up all over the kitchen and just told the angels I had to find that medicine. My daughter's cat Jasmine pawed one of the boxes, and sure enough, there it was!

There are no accidents on planet Earth, so I always find it interesting how people find their special pets—or how their special pets find them. We've all heard stories of how an animal will show up at just the right time, only to become the perfect fit. I think our angels bring these special little creatures to us as our companions and our rewards.

Pets are just one way that the angels communicate to us through animals. One of my clients, whose best friend died in a car accident when they were both twenty-one, says that there have been several times when she was feeling sad or unsettled and has discovered a lovebird sitting on her car and has immediately felt her friend's comforting presence. I have received messages from owls several times. Once I was driving in Montana and saw an owl on the side of the road that had been hit by a truck. I got out and it died in my arms, soft as a kitten. I quickly took it to a taxidermist and had it stuffed to give to my children's school. Ever since, whenever I ask my angels for a sign, I see an owl. Once in Maui I even had a white owl land right on my head. It was a time when I really needed a sign of hope. I got just what I needed.

Seeking guidance from your angels can be very confusing, especially when you first get started. My client Ada Lee came to me to get clarity after asking her angels for a sign about a man who was in her life. She lived in a building with two elevators, and she would ask that a certain elevator arrive first if he was the man for her. That elevator kept coming, but the relationship was not working. What was she doing wrong? She was not being a priestess; she was not demanding an answer. She was just playing, and she was only creating confusion. Her mind was messing with her! I taught her how to ask for her answers. I told her to call upon her guardian angels for a direct message—to ask that they give her a special sign that she personally requests. She asked to see an owl within forty-eight hours if this man was to be her life partner. She did not see one, and within a short time the man she was interested in proposed to another woman. Though Ada Lee didn't really want to believe the message at the time, she now has a way to find her answers.

There are certain things to keep in mind whenever you ask your angels for a sign:

1. Ask to receive your sign within a certain time frame. I ask within forty-eight hours, but many people don't get responses that fast, especially when they're just getting started. You might want to begin by asking to get your sign within three or four days.
2. Ask for what you wish to see. Be specific about what you want your sign to be, then be prepared for it to show up in an unexpected form. As my client with the London job offer revealed, sometimes a ladybug can look like a dog!
3. Be patient and wait; do not seek your sign. Patience is a magic word. You can't force the universe to do things; you have to wait. In the right moment it will happen. By asking for a sign, you have sown the seeds and watered the garden, but the truth takes time to grow. Hurry can be dangerous, because only falsities can be manufactured quickly.

Signs aren't the only requests we must be clear about with our angels. My client Andie wanted to get married, so she asked for a husband. Shortly afterward a neighbor introduced her to a man who was ten years older than she; Andie came to me and said this man was too old. A friend then introduced her to a man who was just her age; Andie came to me and said this man was too young. She met a man at the gym, but he was not ambitious enough; she met a man in her profession, but he worked too hard. You get the picture: instead of asking for what she wanted, Andie was trying to shape it as it came to her. I asked Andie to write a list of a hundred items describing the type of man she wanted to meet. I told her to sit at her magic desk and use pencil and fine paper. The process gave a feel and texture to her desires—so when she met the man of her dreams a few months later, she recognized him. They've been married twelve years now.

When my client Sonja asked her angels for a new car, she kept picturing a Jaguar in the driveway of her house. She did this visualization for three months, until one morning she woke up to find a Jaguar parked in her driveway. The only problem: it belonged to the guest of her neighbor, who had accidentally parked his car in her drive. When she had done the visualization, she had never seen herself driving the car; she had just seen it parked. The takeaway here: get involved in what you imagine. Even if you're focusing on a material desire, you're more likely to get your angels' help if you put some positive emotion behind it and see yourself as happy or at peace. Make yourself an active part of the dream you want your angels to help you achieve. Drive the car!

When you're appealing to your angels, don't ask for something that belongs to someone else. Eileen always saw herself in the house on her corner; eventually she asked her angels to make it hers. A few years later the man who owned the house had to sell it because of illness. Eileen came to me asking if she was in some way responsible. It is possible that she was responsible, but we will never know. It's not good magic to want what someone else has. Ask for something similar or better.

I often think it's best to ask the angels for even more than you want. Shoot for the moon! When I was a little girl, I showed my grandmother my list of the characteristics of the man of my dreams. Grandma Jessie read it and said, "Well, who do you want, Jesus

Christ?" It was the first time that I truly realized the message my family was giving me: *It is too good to be true; you cannot have what you want.* I made the list even better, and now I'm with a man who is everything I could ask for—and more!

Altar Your Life

As eager as your angels are to help you, you can improve your chances of getting what you ask for by using tools and techniques that empower your requests. It's important to make your prayers from your own sacred space—a personal altar that you create in your home. Your altar doesn't have to be large or elaborate to serve as a constant reminder of your wish. Each time you look at your altar, you will remember what you want and be reminded to ask. Staying focused on your wish is what makes it happen!

The word *altar* is derived from the Latin word *altus*, meaning "high and thus exalted." True to its meaning, you will use your altar as the focal point for all ceremonies or rituals. Altars come in all shapes and sizes for different religions, but one thing that seems to be consistent in all faiths is that they ideally will face east, toward the rising sun. There are four items to place on your altar:

- *a cup of water, representing the heart or emotions;*
- *a knife, representing the mind;*
- *a coin, representing the earth or physical world;*
- *a candle, representing fire or the spirit.*

After these basics you can add anything you want, depending on what your wish is. If you need money, for instance, display a picture of what you plan to spend your money on. If you're looking for a life mate, place items on the altar that represent activities you would like to do with another person—matches from a favorite café, for example, or travel brochures for places you want to visit. Use your imagination!

Lighting Your Way

An essential element of any altar is the selection of candles. From building your altar to performing many incantations, candles play a vital role in calling your angels and working your magic. To get the most from your candles, it's important that you choose and prepare them properly.

First, candles must be cleaned to remove any energy influences that may have come into contact with them. Think of all the handling they have had since their creation, and you'll see why you want to clean them. Any soft cloth will do. I always clean my candles with rose water; fresh rainwater is also good to use.

After it has dried, bless the clean candle by holding it in your right hand next to your heart as you say, "Holy angel, I ask you to bless this candle and grant my request." As you bless the candle, focus on feeling the energy going from your heart into the candle.

Next, carve your name and birthdate on the upper part of the candle and anoint your candle with an oil appropriate to your request. Never apply the oil in one stroke; start in the middle and go to the top, then return to the middle and go to the bottom. Clear your mind and concentrate on the purpose of your request as you are rubbing in the oil. The more energy you send into the candle, the better your chances of success.

Candles can be very powerful accessories when you're asking

your angels for help. The basic procedure is the same, whatever you're asking for.

Exercise Your Spirit:	**Ask Your Angels**
What you will need:	**A candle and a desire**
Time:	**As long as you wish**

- *Light the candle.*
- *Get down on your knees, opening up your entire energy field.*
- *Recite the following prayer:*

> *Angels of Light*
> *Angels of Dawn*
> *Bring my desire*
> *And help my life*
> *With your grace I live in peace*
> *I ask you for this on my knees. So be it.*

When you're lighting a candle to ask your angels for help, be sure to choose the color candle that best fits your needs. Each color serves a different purpose:

Red brings physical love and sexual potency and manifests ambitions on a physical level. Red is good for people who do not have a lot of energy, ambition, or drive. It's also good for business deals that don't quite seem to be getting off the ground.

Pink brings attraction, devotion, and love—from romantic love to flirtation to passion. Pink can also bring friendships or be used when dealing with unhappy people.

Blue brings peace, harmony, and protection. The healing power of blue can neutralize bad habits and calm the nerves. Use blue for blessing a house or restoring a broken friendship.

Green draws money, bringing abundance to all areas of life; it is also the color for healing physical disorders and diseases having to do with feminine problems.

Orange has to do with communications. If you're having trouble collecting your thoughts, expressing your desires, making a decision, or just cutting through red tape, orange is the right color. This is a good color for job hunting or pursuing any sort of success.

Purple works for honor, recognition, and acquiring respect. Excellent for business, legal, and professional situations, purple can also help with psychic work. It is a color related to power.

Yellow represents the brilliance of the sun, working wherever a higher consciousness is needed. It also brings happiness, wealth, acclaim, and attention. Yellow can overcome injustices and help turn around a long dismal period in a person's lifestyle; it's also the color ruling marriage.

White is the color of purity: cleansing, purifying, and clearing away obstacles. Use white to clear a path before you when you are making major changes.

Valerie, a Realtor, had always struggled with money, constantly worrying about how she would pay her monthly bills. She made a money candle, using a green candle and bayberry oil, and used the hand prayers I had taught her. I did not see her for almost six months. When she returned, she told me how her luck had changed. She had started selling houses one right after the other. She also admitted to me that she had spilled some of the bayberry oil I had given her in the car she drove whenever she was showing houses. No wonder she sold so many!

This little exercise has helped many clients draw on the power of the candle to attract love.

Exercise Your Spirit: **Burning Love**
What you will need: **Two red candles, oil**
Time: **As long as you wish**

- *Anoint two red candles with an oil you really like.*
- *Carve your name on one candle and leave the other blank.*
- *Place the candles one foot apart and burn them both for one hour.*
- *Over the course of the hour, bring the candles closer together until they are touching each other.*
- *Repeat daily until the candles are done.*

Crystals and Stones

When I was a child, I was always interested in rocks, and my interest just keeps growing. Crystals and stones have been used in ceremonies and in healing by such cultures as the Mayan, Aztec, Native

American, Druid, Celtic, and many African cultures. The Native Americans I have known say that crystals are the storage keepers of the earth. Indeed, each type of crystal has a gift stored inside it for our benefit. The mineral kingdom is here to give us their gifts, and we use them as such: think of our traditions of marriage, for example, in which the gift of a diamond plays such an important role.

No two crystals are ever the same, and each has its own unique history. You activate and amplify the energy of a stone with your touch; by wearing it close to your skin or holding it in your hands, you can use the stone to strengthen your magic or to protect you when you feel weak or tired. Remember that stones store information and energy. When making a gift of a stone that has belonged to someone else—such as an engagement ring that has been in the family—it's best to clear the stone. This can easily be done by placing the stone in sea salt overnight. I've also seen Native American medicine men clear stones by forcefully breathing into them several times, a simple but effective method for cleaning crystals that you can do yourself.

Exercise Your Spirit:	**Cleaning Your Crystal**
What you will need:	**Your crystal**
Time:	**A moment**

- *Hold the crystal in your right hand between your thumb and first two fingers.*
- *Inhale deeply, holding the crystal lightly.*

- **Breathe out through your mouth onto the crystal as fast and as forcefully as you can, as you squeeze the crystal tight.**
- **Repeat three times.**

I have received and passed along many beautiful stones in my life. Stones come into our lives for a time and then sometimes want to move on to another human. They will speak up and let you know: you just need to listen! I keep several crystals in the room with me while I work, as I believe they help with meditation and focusing the mind. They can also be used to provide a psychic shield. To get started, simply hold a clear quartz crystal in your hand and see a protective shield or bubble of light emanating from the pointed end of the crystal.

My client Melanie used this technique while she was living in a home with three other students. When their home was broken into, hers was the only room not entered or vandalized. The roommates, who had given Melanie a hard time about her wacky crystals, later asked her to help them create the same protective shield in their rooms!

I sometimes use a quartz crystal to treat a client's energy field by scanning the body with the crystal and placing an appropriate stone on the client's body. I have seen this procedure open blockages and fill energy holes. I've also seen the blockages and holes return soon after the stones are removed, so I try to leave them in place long enough for a new energy pattern to set into the body. I often send crystals home with clients to use for a period of time, usually one to two weeks.

The clear quartz crystal resonates strongly with the third eye, making it a great stone if you're just getting started working with minerals. I've found that a lot of people come into contact with these stones when they are beginning their spiritual journeys. Once you have your stone, you can use it to practice focusing your energy and your thoughts. So be prepared: there's a stone out there just waiting for you!

Exercise Your Spirit:	Chakra Scan
What you will need:	A quartz crystal
Time:	20 minutes

- *Breathe on the crystal to clear it.*
- *As you hold the crystal in your left hand, connect to the crystal with your sixth chakra (third eye).*
- *Move from your third eye through the crystal to your healing angels.*
- *Point the sharp end of the crystal into your chakras, taking note of how you feel as you point the crystal into your body.*
- *If you feel something unusual in a particular chakra, then explore that chakra some more with the exercises that relate to it in chapter four.*
- *Write down your experience and repeat it in forty-eight hours.*

To get to know more about how your crystal responds to energy, ask a friend if you can use your crystal to do a chakra scan on them as well. Quartz crystals have been used in healing for centuries. In medieval times, for example, a small quartz crystal was placed against the tongue to bring down a fever or to diminish thirst.

The next exercise shows you how to program your crystal for love. You can adapt the same technique to bring about any kind of result—attracting money, finding work, having a child, breaking a habit, increasing your spiritual knowledge, and so on.

Exercise Your Spirit: **Inside Your Stone**
What you will need: **A quartz crystal**
Time: **10 minutes**

- *Hold your crystal in your right hand, squeezing it between your thumb and first two fingers.*
- *In your mind's eye, go inside your crystal and stand inside it, with your arms stretched out touching the point of the crystal.*
- *Say out loud,* I am love *(or* I am wealthy, I am pregnant, etc.).
- *Fill the inside of the crystal with all the love in your heart.*
- *Walk out of the crystal and back into your physical body.*
- *Squeeze your crystal three times and say,* Oh holy stone, serve my life of love. *(Or* Oh holy stone, serve my life of abundance, *or* Oh holy stone, serve my life of mothering, etc.)

While you can use the same stone to get different results, each variety of stone has its own unique attributes; as you get more advanced in your magic, you will want to work with stones that are particularly well suited to bringing about the results you want. Organized by the chakras stones relate to, the following guide to stones and their qualities connects each stone to the desires you want to enforce, the flowers that activate the stones, the hours at which they are most powerful (both a.m. and p.m.), and the planets whose influence they call upon.

First Chakra

Planet: Saturn   Flower: hyacinth   Hour: 1:00

Smoky Quartz: Strengthens survival instincts and neutralizes energies that are harmful to the body (such as radiation or emissions from electromagnetic fields). Use this stone to do magic exercises that bring you material stability and to heal issues from early childhood.

Agate: Builds confidence, self-esteem, and courage; strengthens eyesight and promotes marital fidelity. In the past, agate was placed in water for use in cooking and drinking to dispel sickness.

Second Chakra

Planet: Mars   Flower: Tuberose   Hour: 2:00

Amber: Brings magnetism, stimulates fertility and creative forces, and helps breathing and memory. I feel that this fossilized resin balances the nervous system of the body; because I use my nervous system so much in my work, I often wear a small green amber cross, which seems to draw people to it on those rare occasions that I wear it outside of work.

Third Chakra

   Planet: Moon   Flower: Gardenia   Hour: 3:00

Unakite: Balances emotions and brings feelings of peace.

Marble: Calms the emotional body.

Alabaster: Promotes forgiveness and helps the body feel centered.

Fourth Chakra

   Planet: Venus   Flower: Primrose   Hour: 4:00

Rose quartz: Promotes self-love and increases love magic.

Ruby: The master gem of the heart, promotes joy and love.

Fifth Chakra

   Planet: Mercury   Flower: Violet Hour: 5:00

Turquoise: Develops wisdom, aids communication.

Aquamarine: Fosters independence and creativity; clears negative thought forms and enhances energy flow.

Sixth Chakra

   Planet: Moon   Flower: Iris   Hour: 6:00

Opal: Enhances intuition.
Pearl: Adds a sparkle to intuition and clairvoyance.

Seventh Chakra

Planet: Pluto   Flower: Sunflower   Hour: 7:00

Amethyst: Taps into male spiritual energy—a good thing to do when you become a bit dreamy and need to get things done. Many bishops in the Catholic Church wear amethyst rings, both for their protective powers and for the energy they bring to meditation. The stone of spirituality and contentment, amethyst also helps transmute negative energy and release old emotional pain, so it's useful when you are feeling overly emotional and want to heal the past. It can even help treat addictions and promote good sleep.

Eighth Chakra

Planet: Earth   Flower: Goldenrod   Hour: 8:00

Rutilated Quartz: Helps amplify and broadcast information, so wear it when you are ready to be heard. Also stimulates brain function, inspiration, and clairvoyance; strengthens the immune system; and eases melancholy.

Aventurine: Increases luck or chance.

Topaz: Brings success to all endeavors.

Ninth Chakra

Planet: Uranus   Flower: Pansy   Hour: 9:00

Sapphire: Calms the nerves, attracts beneficial influences, and strengthens faith.

Tenth Chakra

Planet: Neptune   Flower: Chrysanthemum   Hour: 10:00

Citrine: Promotes concentration and clear thinking. Citrine is an unusual mineral in that it transmutes negative energy instead of holding or accumulating it; as a result, it never needs clearing or cleansing. Known through history as the "merchant's stone," citrine is also very good for acquiring and maintaining money. Call upon the angel of accumulation when you use this stone.

Lapis Lazuli: Attracts wisdom and helps surpass limitations.

Eleventh Chakra

Planet: Jupiter   Flower: Lily of the valley   Hour: 11:00

Ametrine: Balances male/female energies, enhances universal equilibrium, and helps people understand their path. A mixture of citrine and amethyst, this is my favorite stone. Ametrine provides a clear connection between the physical form and the ultimate state of perfection. Holding it during meditation helps me reach a higher state, and I always feel better when I use it!

Twelfth Chakra

Planet: Sun   Flower: Rose   Hour: 12:00

Diamond: Resonates with the vibration of joy.

Phosphorite: Stimulates spiritual growth, attracting great knowledge and bringing joy for the journey.

Once you know what stone to use, you can add it to many of the exercises throughout the book. You can use the right stone to increase the power of your magic by holding it or wearing it, as in a piece of jewelry, or even a rosary. I will also sometimes use a gemstone to make an elixir—a liquid that is basically water with the essence of something (in this case a stone) that can enhance your desires when you're doing your magic. In the following recipe, you can also add an ounce of brandy at the end, to stabilize and maintain the frequencies. If you include the brandy, store the final tonic in a dark colored bottle; when you use it, place only two or three drops under your tongue. Without the brandy you can just drink the elixir as you would water.

Exercise Your Spirit:	**Magic Elixir**
What you will need:	**A gemstone of your choice, one gallon of distilled water, a glass jar or bowl, one ounce of brandy (optional)**
Time:	**48 hours**

- *Select your gemstone, depending on what you want to accomplish:*

  - *To bring money: citrine, topaz, emerald, or jade*
  - *To attract love: rose quartz, ruby, pink tourmaline, rutile*

- *To attain clarity: diamond, obsidian, citrine*
- *To balance your chakras: chrysocolla*

- *Clean the gemstone well.*
- *Place the stone in the glass container (no metal should be used).*
- *Place it in the sun- and moonlight for at least forty-eight hours.*

The Power of the Talisman

One of your most powerful tools for calling on the universe can be a talisman you create yourself. The word *talisman* originates from the Greek word *teleo,* meaning "to consecrate." Through this process of consecration, you can convert images into an effective instrument of your will.

Always construct your talisman with a specific result in mind. You need to be able to write the exact nature of your objective down in a single sentence; any ambiguity can leave room for the talisman to fail or even backfire. The chart below lists the main spheres of influence that are likely to describe your objective. From this chart you can learn the planet involved with your objective—an important fact to know, because your talisman will be linked with that planetary force. You'll also see the best day of the week for your objective, as well as the fragrances to help you charge your talisman; fragrances affect your central nervous system and your auric field, adding yet another resource to your collection of tools for communicating with the universe. The chart of the days of the week on page xx can provide additional necessary information.

- **Earth** *(Friday): Objective: health, establishment, death, agriculture, legacies, sorrow, solidification, and materializing anything you have been wanting. Fragrances: sage, patchouli, orange.*
- **Saturn** *(Saturday): Objective: honor, riches, apparel, position. Fragrances: hyacinth, iris, patchouli, violet.*
- **Jupiter** *(Thursday): Objective: expansion, knowledge, fortune, gold, rulership. Fragrances: lime, sandalwood.*
- **Mars** *(Tuesday): Objective: energy, legal cases. Fragrances: coconut, gardenia, honeysuckle, carnation, pine, myrrh.*
- **Venus** *(Friday): Objective: love, music, pleasure, luxury. Fragrances: rose, vanilla, cherry.*
- **Mercury** *(Wednesday): Objective: books, learning, writing, communication. Fragrances: bayberry, lemongrass, lavender.*
- **Moon** *(Monday): Objective: dreams, change, childbirth, reproduction, psychic matters. Fragrances: rose, musk.*

Exercise Your Spirit:	Create Your Own Talisman
What you will need:	A piece of cloth about 18 inches square, a candle, ribbon, and incense of the fragrance

	to match your desire, a pencil, paper, maga zines, scissors, salt
Time:	Take as much as you wish

Building the Talisman:
- *Write your wish in pencil on a piece of paper.*
- *Sign and date the paper.*
- *Cut pictures depicting your wish out of magazines and pile them on the paper on top of each other on the cloth.*

Charging the Talisman:
- *Place the piece of cloth with the visual images that you cut out in front of you. This will be your talisman.*
- *Visualize a large, luminous sphere of your favorite color above the talisman.*
- *State your written intention out loud in a single sentence.*
- *Sprinkle the talisman with water, saying,* I consecrate this talisman with water to the end that it may . . . , *and repeat your intention again.*
- *Light the scented incense and pass the talisman through its smoke, saying,* I consecrate this talisman with fire to the end that it may . . . , *and repeat your intention again.*
- *Breathe upon the talisman several times, saying,* I consecrate this talisman with air to the end that it may . . . , *and repeat your intention again.*

- *Sprinkle the talisman with salt, saying,* I consecrate this talisman with earth to the end that it may . . . , *and repeat your intention again.*
- *Visualize the colored sphere descending into the talisman and becoming part of it, as you say,* I consecrate this talisman with my life to the end that it may . . . , *and repeat your intention again.*
- *Fold or roll up the cloth with everything inside it, set it aside in a safe place, and extinguish the incense. Seal the wrapped talisman with wax and tie it with ribbon.*
- *Hide the talisman and forget it. It's essential that you forget about your talisman, because constant worry or conjecture about the process can interfere with the magic.*

A talisman should work well enough that its effectiveness is obvious within seven days of its blessing. Once it is created and charged, it can be left to do its work without further attention; if the blessing has been carried out correctly, your talisman will automatically recharge itself, rather like a rechargeable battery. Four clients did this exercise together and all reported results in less than the seven days! One wanted her boyfriend of seven years to propose; he had told her on so many occasions that he did not want to get married that she was ready to give up, but three days after her exercise he proposed and they went ring shopping! Another one wanted to get promoted at work and within a few days was interviewed for a better position that was hers one month later! It is fun when you do a spring cleaning and find these little bundles full of your dreams. If your dream has come true, you can open them and disperse the energy back to the heavens. Shake the cloth and then give it to someone who needs what you received.

With the forces of the heavens and the universe within your reach, your magic is more powerful than ever. Now it's time to share it with others. The next key will show ways for you to do just that.

CHAPTER 7

KEY 7: Share the Magic

Spread love everywhere you go. Let no one ever come to you without leaving happier.

—MOTHER TERESA

Magic isn't something that you hold on to. It isn't yours to keep; it's yours to share. Our love and our blessings don't come to us: they move through us, touching the lives of others before and after us just as they touch our own. That's the wonderful thing about magic: the more you share it, the more you have in your life.

We have now come to the key that will truly unlock the gate to your magical life. The inner world functions by different laws than the material world. The idea that if you give it, you lose it, doesn't apply to magic. With magic—as with kindness, with joy, and with love—the more you give, the more you receive. Magic is not a business and can't be shared with conditions or expectations. Give your magic without any strings attached—asking nothing in return, just giving for the joy of giving—and the Law of Cause and Effect will take care of the rest. You will receive far more than you give.

Another universal law, the Law of Energy, reminds us that we're all connected. When you live your magical life, you create a space in which others can change and grow. By sharing your magic, you give other people the chance to find their own magic. And once they do, they share their magic as well—with you and with everyone else. This is how our magic flows through us and out to others and then comes back to us, multiplied. It costs nothing to be kind and loving, and it brings so much back to you. Holding back does not change lives; taking risks and living from the heart are what make the difference.

All of us belong to the same human family, sharing the same home here on earth. Our home represents the element we are closest to. When we are walking, sleeping, working at our jobs, and tending our gardens, we are working within the element of earth— the realm of abundance and stability, the element upon which the other three rest. We call on the strength and healing of the earth element as we invite it to be part of our journey:

Exercise Your Spirit:	Earth Blessing
What you will need:	You
Time:	10 to 15 minutes

- *Press your hand into fresh dirt and feel its fertility.*
- *Know that upon its surface we live our lives; within its surface we raise our food; beneath its surface we bury our deceased.*

- *Repeat this call out loud:*

Oh Dear Earth

Feel my feet upon your face
On you I join the human race

The tree brings fruit right to my hands
Help me dance upon the land

Sun will shine and wind will blow
The earth supports me, this I know

Oh sweet earth, please guide my heart
Bring me home to find my part

- *Feel your feet upon the earth.*
- *For the next five minutes, touch anything you can get your hands on!*

Although they are both called earth, the element and the planet are not the same thing. Our planet is simply a manifestation of the stable, solid energy of the element, which also exists within us and within the universe at large. Once you are more aware of your connection to the earth, it's easier to get in touch with your love for the planet and for the people you share it with. You can do this indoors or outside, by filling your heart chakra with loving earth energy. The mantra that helps you do this is the same mantra I heard, beating like a drum, when the Mother visited me in my hospital room when I was called into my work.

Exercise Your Spirit:	Earth Heart
What you will need:	Your wand
Time:	10 to 15 minutes

- *Sit in a comfortable place.*
- *As you breathe deeply, imagine that with each breath a root grows from your first chakra (at the base of your spine) down into the core of the earth.*
- *Now feel earth energy flowing into you with each breath, until it fills your entire body.*
- *Bring your awareness to your heart chakra, and open yourself up to be filled with yellow-gold cosmic energy.*
- *Allow the two energies to mix and fill your body.*
- *Holding your magic wand in your right hand, repeat this mantra as you move your wand in a clockwise motion:*

Earth heart earth heart earth heart

- *Notice that the letters, when written, fit together:*

Eartheartearthearteartheartheartheart.

Like the beat of your heart, the universe is a constant flow. Unless your mind gets in the way, the universe always gives you the same amount of energy and always will, without holding back. While there are times that we may think that the universe gives us more—when we think that there is just too much to do,

ancient ritual. But many people tell me that the traditions they grew up with have lost their relevance and their appeal. Instead of bringing people together and giving meaning to life, the customs of modern holidays sometimes leave many people feeling isolated, empty, or depressed.

The need to join together and align our energies never goes away, however. We are naturally drawn to holidays that unite people of like minds so we can share our magic and our love. I celebrate holidays by holding prayer and meditation services. One of my favorite meditations is one you can do on your own:

Exercise Your Spirit:	**Globe Meditation**
What you will need:	**You**
Time:	**10 to 15 minutes**

- *Take a moment to sit in silence and let your mind become very still.*
- *Feel your body, paying attention to its solidness.*
- *Notice your heartbeat, and feel the flow of energy in your body.*
- *Center yourself and let your thoughts be still as you focus on a light that enters the room.*
- *See this light as a globe.*
- *In your mind's eye, move the globe of light and place it in front of you so that you can step right into it.*
- *Step in and out of the globe three times.*
- *Breathe the globe into your heart and let it drift down into your body between your solar plexus and navel.*

- *Think of a question you have been waiting for an answer to.*
- *Ask your question, and as you ask it, see your words go up in smoke.*
- *Let the smoke be carried to the angels.*
- *See a flaming arrow return back and go through your body and into the earth.*
- *This arrow drops down to the base of your spine.*
- *Let the fire flame up your spine and burn up anything unnecessary in your mind.*
- *Let the past go. Feel your core get stronger.*

This meditation prepares you for another ritual of celebration, the Eucharist. Christianity is not the only spiritual discipline that draws upon the natural sacramental power of eating and drinking for ritual. The physical acts of eating and drinking are central to the way we maintain and understand human life. Drinking is one of the first things we do; eating together seems to be deeply embedded in the human psyche as a way to build and celebrate unity. And from magical understanding to modern proverbs, we get the sense that, as the saying goes, "You are what you eat." All of these connotations are present in the ritual of the Eucharist, which gets its name from the Greek word *eucharistia*, meaning "thanksgiving."

While you may associate the Eucharist with very specific rites of the Christian church, you can actually perform your own version to give thanks at home. When bread and wine are taken, blessed, and shared, the participants join together in deep understanding of the elements' symbolic significance: the wine symbolizes the blood that brings life as it runs through our bodies, while the bread represents the earth and our physical bodies. You can bless the meal by visualizing a golden ball of light coming from the sun and into your body while you hold the chalice of wine; as the light passes through your hands and into the chalice, it infuses the wine with all that you desire. You and everyone present are thus joined together to manifest all aspects of your lives—social, economic, political, and creative.

Exercise Your Spirit:	**Giving Thanks**
What you will need:	**A cup or chalice, red wine or grape juice, small pieces of bread or wafers**
Time:	**10 to 15 minutes**

- *Place the food and drink on your altar or on a table where all can see it. Everyone present will bless the wine by holdling their hands out and imaging the sun shining through their bodies and out of their hands into the beverage.*
- *Think of all that you desire your life to be.*
- *Think of all that you desire your community to be.*
- *Think of all that you desire your world to be socially, economically, politically, and personally.*
- *Take turns first eating a piece of bread and then drinking the blessed liquid.*

- *Say a prayer of thanks at the end, such as*

Thank you for all that we receive, all that we are, and all that we shall be. Amen.

You Are Your Birthday

Most of us already celebrate our birthdays, but when you get in touch with your magic, you may start to change the way you do so. Birthdays don't always have to be about receiving gifts; I like to celebrate my birthdays by both giving and receiving. Your birthday can also be a celebration of all that has happened over the past year, and a time to dream and create your next year. The night before my birthday I bathe in Epsom salts to purify my body. I then dress in white and light a yellow or gold candle on my altar for vision and illumination. I place photos of my parents and grandparents on the altar with some flowers around them, thanking them for life and all lessons learned. I thank all my ancestors who have passed before me and ask for their guidance in the year ahead.

I will often invite people who have influenced my year into my home to give them small gifts that acknowledge their role in making my year meaningful and successful. The food and drink I serve depend on what I want to celebrate.

Cake is for celebration and can be combined with any of the following depending on your intention:

Citrus foods: joy and vitality
Fruit: abundance, health, potential
Chocolate: sexuality and creativity
Milk: nurturing sustenance

Pomegranate: rebirth, abundance

Sunflower seeds: new potential

Wine and grape juice: celebration, bounty, and wealth (red wine
to honor women, white wine to honor men)

Your birthday is also a good time to celebrate and reflect upon
the attributes that come from being born on that particular day. I'm
speaking, of course, about the insight into your personality and fortunes that can be gained from knowing your astrological profile. Astrology is one of the world oldest sciences; star charts by Egyptian
astrologers have been dated as far back as 4200 BC. For thousands
of years people have believed that the position of the planets at the
time of their birth determines how they look and act, what they like
and excel at, even whom they are and are not compatible with.

Learning about astrology takes time and practice; fortunately
the resources are vast, so it's easy and fun to begin developing astrology as yet another tool for understanding yourself and your
path. Because I know I was born under the sign of Virgo, I celebrate
the planet Mercury, which rules my sign and influences writing and
communications. I honor that side of my self each year on my birthday by making a list of people I'd like to meet and things I'd like to
accomplish in the following year. I write this list in my magic notebook, where I can easily find it whenever I want to look back and
see that each year much of what I ask comes true!

The Life of the Magus

As you have probably noticed, many of the rituals and traditions with which we celebrate our holidays do more than just bring
people closer to each other: they also bring people closer to their

magic. Of course, those effects are interrelated: true magi know that they must never stop developing their magic if they want to share it, and must never stop sharing their magic if they want to develop it. They also understand that magic is expressed not only in what they do but also in how they live. You share your magic by living the life you were born to live, by finding your purpose and fulfilling your destiny. You also share your magic by attaining the essential characteristics of a magical life: confidence, cooperation, authenticity, vulnerability, intimacy, joy, and generosity. Develop them through practice and trust, and you will have everything you'll need on the path to the life of your dreams.

Confidence is the foundation of a magical life. You must have confidence in your magic and in the perfection of the world. The way you live demonstrates what you believe, so it's important that you believe in the good. We all become either teachers of hope and possibility or teachers of fear and loss. Have confidence in your magic, and you'll be a messenger of hope.

To get to the level of completely trusting your magic, you may first have to go through a period of rethinking and realigning your life. You may experience some changes or reconsider your values. Your old life will look different: when you experience the power of your magic, you'll see how much you used to limit yourself, and you'll want to put those restrictions behind you. Now that you can use all your magic, there's nothing that can hold you back!

While some clients just sail through the changes in their lives, others say that they have to let go of the old before their new life arrives. I've had clients who lose their jobs or end unrewarding relationships; I have watched them leave their designer clothes habits behind or spend less time with people who partied and gossiped and more quality time with family. As my client Frances opened up to her magic, she began to question her friendships; suddenly her best friend said she didn't want to be friends anymore. Frances was in shock, but a few months after their falling out she realized how much more energy she now had for other interests. Her friend had actually been taking up her best time, calling up to five times a day to gossip and complain about her life. It was more of an addiction than a real friendship. Now Frances has several close friends who give back positive energy.

You will receive whatever you need to align yourself to your true purpose, but sometimes you must give up what you have before you get what you need. If you have put too much value on other people and things, for example, you may be given the opportunity to let go of them. You may even feel that you're being forced to do it and respond with worry or fear. Stay confident in your magic, and you'll find that you still hold on to what matters most.

Exercise Your Spirit:	**Letting Go**
What you will need:	**You**
Time:	**10 minutes**

- *Make a list of whom or what you need to let go of.*
- *Close your eyes and see how you would act, look, and be if you let go of them.*
- *Feel how it would feel to be free of these things.*
- *Own the feeling.*
- *Declare it:* **So be it.**
- *Hand the list over to your angels and ask them for help. Tear up the list and wash your hands.*

It takes confidence and learning to trust that all things, events, en-counters, and circumstances are magical and therefore for your good. Once you understand that you create your life—that you have the magic inside you—you will enter a period when you set-tle into a wonderful sense of peace. At this point you begin to gather your magical companions. You'll watch as you begin to find your life moving with more grace.

Cooperation comes with the knowledge that the world is all con-nected and depends on everyone's working together. When you co-operate, you're no longer resisting the world; you now have your magic and you want to be with others and share your life. You let down your defenses and become gentle, giving yourself permission to engage in those simple acts of caring that can make an enormous difference in others' lives.

Think of those situations in which you have allowed yourself to be caring and cooperative. They may have seemed like "chance" meetings, but there is really no such thing: each of these encounters has the potential to become a life-changing experience. Sometimes we can just offer a smile or a helping hand, while other times those gifts will be just what we need from someone else.

I received a clear reminder of this principle one busy after-noon at a large discount grocery store. It was a typical, crowded day with many people darting around with full carts looking for that "shorter" line or that "faster" clerk. I found my place in line, and within a few moments an older gentleman had joined the line behind me. I had loaded some very heavy bottles in my cart, and I was unsure whether I'd be able to pull them out and place them on the checkout counter. When I finally reached the checkout, the "angel" behind me—instantly came to my aid, unasked, lifting the heavy items from my cart. When I noticed he was holding only one small bag of candy, I suggested that he go ahead of me, but he refused. I told the clerk to add his candy to my bill and left the market. The gentleman followed me out to my car to thank me, loaded all the groceries into my car, and told me how much his grandchildren would enjoy that candy. Now, I will probably never see that man again, but it does not matter. We had a sweet encounter and both of us left happier. Even at the level of the most casual encounter it is possible for two people to lose sight of separate interests, if only for a moment.

The next day I had a totally different experience. I walked my little dog to the local knitting store to check on some yarn I had ordered. There was no sign prohibiting dogs, so I didn't think it would be a problem to bring my dog in with me. The owner of the store, whom I had never met, quickly told me that I could not bring my dog in. I apologized and asked if she would mind if I stood by the door while she checked on my order. She rudely ordered me out of her store and told me she would not even answer my question until the dog was outside. I did not leave the store with a good feeling, and I'm sure she didn't feel good about it either, having just lost a customer and potential friend. I actually went back to see if I could find out where this outburst had come from and was treated badly again. So I had to let go. I went elsewhere, and we both lost.

To be cooperative, we give our time, our energy, and our consideration. What keeps us from giving those things freely is often our fear. Of course, there is no reason to fear giving of ourselves. This little exercise can help you remember that's it's okay to give freely. The fruit at the end puts you in touch with the healing power of earth energy.

Exercise Your Spirit:	**Nothing to Fear**
What you will need:	**A piece of fruit**
Time:	**10 to 15 minutes**

- *Relax, close your eyes, and breathe a deep, calming breath.*
- *In your mind's eye, let a picture arise that shows you in a beautiful setting in a state of complete fulfillment.*
- *Hold on to that picture as you repeat a few deep breaths.*
- *When you're finished, eat a piece of fresh fruit and say*

   Life gives me all I need to be completely happy.

Authenticity means living a life that honestly connects body, mind, and soul. Jenna worked as a chef for a famous actor for almost ten years. She did not agree with many of the things she was asked to do or with the way he treated women, but she put up with things because she loved cooking and he was very kind to her. She knew in her heart that on an important level it just didn't feel right, and after she was asked one last time to do something that didn't feel authentic, she finally quit. It was the end of her job, but the beginning of her magical journey. Now Jenna does healing work, using her very powerful gift to help others. She is connected to her magic with body, mind, and soul, and she's always telling me how peaceful her life is—and how authentic it feels.

You can be more authentically connected to your magic if you cultivate your sense of being a source for good. This sense can be strengthened with four simple steps:

1. See magic: Remember that everything in life is magic, and refuse to see anything else. Forget about "the good, the bad, and the ugly": the bad and the ugly are an illusion, a projection of fear. The good is truth and is waiting for you. By now you know that you don't just accidentally run into magic; you expect it, see it and make it real.

2. Believe in magic when you do not see it: There are days when magic is just not as obvious, when we cannot get out of our minds to see it; these are the days when we need to believe in magic in our hearts. Sometimes we have to work extra hard to expect it or believe in it. The effect is always well worth it.

3. Think about magic when you have trouble believing in it: This is one time when going to the past can be valuable—to find a memory of a magical experience from the past to recall when the present doesn't look as bright.

4. Imagine magic when you cannot think of it: Our imagination is a powerful tool. You have been practicing and mastering its techniques; this is an excellent way to put it to use!

When you are in touch with your sense of being a source of magic, you share that blessing with everyone around you. Here's a simple exercise that shows you how:

Exercise Your Spirit:	Brighten Someone's Day
What you will need:	**A yellow candle**
Time:	**10 to 15 minutes**

- *Light a yellow candle.*
- *Invite a higher force—whether that be God, the Mother, Jesus, or Buddha—to join you in the exercise.*
- *Bless everything in your life and know that it is for your good.*
- *Take a few minutes and receive into your body the light that the earth is receiving from our beloved sun.*
- *Tell someone you love to do the same.*

Our **vulnerability** can also hold the key to our strength. I have a painting by a dear friend, Chris Binnion, of a large rose surrounded by the saying, "*Al Ser Vulnerable, Me Vuelo Invincible*" ("In my vulnerability is my invincibility"). Though the words are in Spanish, the message is for all who enter my office. My client Jacquie certainly got the message: she came to me after being hurt many times, determined never to be hurt again. But as she discovered her magic, she dropped her shield and realized that everything she had experienced was in fact the source of her strength—that she had created what she considered her hardships so that she could learn from them and grow.

Vulnerability is an essential element of **intimacy**, which grows in importance as you get deeper into your magic. While intimacy may have seemed threatening in the past, your magic unlocks your desire to really be known on the deepest level. Now that you have your magic, you will want to find your mate. Throughout this book are techniques that have helped many people—men and women—find true love. If you're still waiting to try them, there's no reason to wait any longer! It's never too late to start trying; my client Jody had sworn off dating for five years, but after discovering and using her magic she soon found her life partner.

Joy is the state you attain when you know that everything is perfect—that you have nothing to fear. Our magic helps us receive more and more of what we ask for. The abundance we create and receive is ours to enjoy! If you do not trust life, you cannot place your life in the hands of joy.

I have found that many people consider it harder to receive than to give. A few years ago I was speaking about this concept to a group when a woman in the back of the room called out, "If that is true, then give me that ring you are wearing." I was wearing a large topaz ring that had been given me by a beloved friend whose spiritual journey has always inspired me. As I continued speaking, I slipped the ring off my finger and threw it right into the lap of the woman who had asked for it.

I have learned that this world of ours is incredibly abundant, and that the riches we think we own are really only entrusted to us for a short time, so it was easy for me to give the ring away. But it was hard for the woman in back to accept it; she sat there squirming, in obvious discomfort, as I finished my talk. Afterward she came up to me and handed me the ring, saying, "I cannot receive this." It was as easy for me to accept it as it had been to give it away. "I am sorry that you cannot accept it," I replied, "but every time I wear it I will think of you and see you learning to receive."

The difficulty that people sometimes have accepting what they ask for can develop into a general uneasiness with success. Some people fear success and abundance because they observe that wealth often brings unhappiness and a loss of spiritual motivation. It doesn't have to be this way. The real proof of spirituality is in the world; a spirituality that cannot withstand temptations—such as money—is not a deeply rooted spirituality anyway.

It's true that money and success can be invasive, but only when they usurp all other priorities. Meditation helps ensure a balance in our life between the spiritual and the material. When you stay in touch with your magic, and surrender to love in all its forms, you can maintain the balance you need to find a healthy joy in your success.

When success is a source of joy, it can actually create more room for further spiritual development. If it takes all a person's time to meet the daily necessities of life, there will be less time for spiritual contemplation. The satisfaction of material needs can be a spiritual act when it is a means rather than an end unto itself— a step in the process of creating a life that allows one to turn to higher aspirations. In this sense, poverty can represent a greater possible threat to spirituality than wealth.

Do you have the fear that money and power corrupt? Try repeating this affirmation: *I love all that source gives.* Approach success slowly and deliberately but with great forcefulness and energy. Be steadfast in purpose and yet playful at the same time. Playfulness is an important characteristic of the magical life, because most people take their lives way too seriously. The magic keys teach us that it's OK to play again—and that life gets better when we do.

Don't be afraid to ask for what you need. This exercise can draw on the power of bayberry oil—a scent that promotes sharing and abundance—to help you both receive more and give more to others. As you'll see, sharing the magic is an essential element of making it work!

Exercise Your Spirit:	**Drawing Money**
What you will need:	**A green candle, paper, bayberry oil**
Time:	**20 minutes**

- *Carve your name and birthday on a green candle with a key.*
- *Rub some bayberry oil onto the candle.*
- *Using your magic pencil, write the amount of money you need for a specific purpose (perhaps a bill or a holiday gift) on a square of white paper.*
- *Place the paper beneath the green candle.*
- *Burn the candle for fifteen minutes each day until the candle is gone.*
- *Give this ceremony to a friend.*

Finally, **generosity** reminds us that sharing our abundance is as important as accepting it. We give in order to live with grace. When we fail to give, we make it harder to receive the abundance of the universe. I was given a vivid reminder of this one day on the streets of New York City, when I ran into a friend who complimented me on the hat I was wearing. It was one of my favorite hats, and when she asked to borrow it, I didn't want to share it. I said no, walked about three steps, and then felt the wind blow the hat right off of my head. I turned around just in time to see it run over by a New York City bus! Right there on the sidewalk, I said that I would never again hold anything back.

Another powerful lesson of the value of generosity came in an apparition, when the Holy Mother asked me to give away everything I owned that I couldn't fit in a single suitcase. I bought a superlarge suitcase to fill and gave everything else away, including my car. To this day, whenever I return to Idaho, I see people wearing my clothes or jewelry. It often brings me more joy to see those items on others than it did to claim them as mine, and the whole experience has taught me how unnecessary most things are. More importantly, I received an ongoing lesson in the abundance of the world. Though I gave everything away, I have never gone without anything I need: I have always been taken care of in every way.

Being generous is the yoga of the soul: it gives us a chance to stretch. It is easy to give away something that you're tired of; try giving something away that you really love or really think you need. It is a powerful stretch. Think about how attached you are to your favorite possessions. How much would you want to have them if you only had a few months to live? Would it really matter who had them once you were gone? What you'll find if you do give something precious away is that you stretch your spirit by giving. Attachments to things can be extremely limiting. When we let them go, our spirits can grow.

One reason you can afford to be generous is the simple fact of your abundance. You are endlessly wealthy. You have created every situation in your life, and with each moment you create your future. The wealth in your hands is yours to do with what you like. This exercise draws on the power of the earth element to give life force to your inner riches.

Exercise Your Spirit: **Grow Your Riches**

What you will need: A clay pot, potting soil, a bulb, paper

Time: ongoing

- *Write down on a single piece of paper all the qualities that constitute your inner riches.*
- *Wrap the paper around the bulb and plant it in the soil.*
- *Keep the plant watered and watch it grow.*
- *The roots and shoots of the bulb will grow right through your riches, allowing them to break through the surface and reach up toward the sun.*

Several of my clients are very wealthy financially, but they don't all deal with their affluence in the same way. Mitzi is blessed with monetary wealth but has no joy in her life. She counts her pennies and worries that anyone who dates her is only after her money. She is constantly returning things; once she even refused to pay for an elaborate, custom birthday cake she had ordered because she insisted that its marzipan caricature didn't look enough like her—even though everyone at the party said otherwise. Most of her nights she spends at home, alone, watching movies in her private home theater. She does not share her magic.

Another client, Toni, is just as wealthy but shares what she has with joy and celebration. The people in her life are always receiving gifts, and Toni seems to know what they need before they even need it. Where Mitzi has trouble keeping any staff, Toni has a large staff at home who are happy to be serving her. She is generous and kind to everyone she encounters, and she receives a true generosity of spirit in return. Toni truly shares her magic and is regarded as a wonderful role model by all who know her.

Among the biggest differences between Mitzi and Toni are their views of the abundance of the world. Mitzi fears that there is a limit to the bounty of the universe, where Toni understands the boundlessness of the plenty that surrounds her. Mitzi fears that to give is to lose, while Toni understands that to give is to receive.

When we understand that giving is receiving, we have learned one of the most beautiful and powerful lessons of a magical life. A few years ago on Christmas Eve I was given a beautiful holy relic of Saint Ann, the mother of the Virgin Mary. I didn't grow up Catholic, so I didn't even know these things existed, but I knew it was special and I loved it with all my heart. A month later one of my clients came in and saw it. She asked, "What is that?" but what I heard her say inside was "I want that." I gave it to her without a thought. Since that day I have received over twenty holy relics into my sacred trust. But I don't know that I would have received even a second relic if I hadn't so freely given the first.

I told a client about this experience, and she gave an opal ring to a woman she had just met. Her purpose in giving was not to receive—she had simply heard that she should give the ring to that woman—but ten days later her grandmother gave her a beautiful sapphire ring that the grandmother had been given as a girl. All it took was for my client to trust that the world is an abundant place. Once she moved into the flow of the universe, her magic naturally spread.

Yvonne came to see me because she was struggling with

money. She wanted to do something meaningful with her life but felt trapped in what she felt was a meaningless job. She did not feel that she could afford to just quit her job and seek her spiritual work. She had lost sight of the fact that everything is spiritual and had lost touch with her faith in the abundance of the universe; she was limiting herself with her belief system.

I told her to start tithing—to give 10 percent of her income to a noble charitable cause or just to someone she knew who really was struggling. At the same time, I introduced her to bayberry, which brings money and blessings to those who daily anoint their wrists with it. You can sprinkle your billfold or purse once a week with this legendary scent and never be without money. Three weeks after Yvonne started using bayberry and gave some money to an organization for starving children, she was offered a new job within her company—a job that not only brought a 40 percent raise but also involved working closely with a foundation she has always respected. Yvonne gave her way to a new level of material and spiritual abundance!

Finding Your Purpose

The ultimate expression of generosity is to find your purpose and live your dream. You fulfill your destiny by drawing on all the magic you have developed and freely sharing it with the world. When you live the life you were born to live, you finally make yourself whole. It is the biggest gift you can give yourself and your world, and it will bring you the greatest and most profound rewards.

You have come far enough in your magic that it is now time to decide how you want to use it. What do you want in your life? You have the power to create the life of your dreams. It is up to you to decide what that life will look like, and what it will include.

This is often easier said than done. As you have deepened your magic, you've probably gotten in touch with more aspects of your self; you may have realized that you have so many facets to your personality that it's hard to decide what you want your role in life to be. One useful strategy is to list and prioritize your interests, and then seek some activity that incorporates the key interests in a more stimulating and productive way. Another approach is to seek out an important unmet need of a segment of society; if you are the one who sees the need, chances are that you are also meant to fulfill it.

You Never Dream an Impossible Dream

Have you ever felt that you were on the verge of success but couldn't quite see the next step? Or do you feel you have the potential to be fabulously wealthy but can't see the clear path to realize your potential? You may already have some of the answers you're looking for: it's just that you're not awake when they come to you! Our dreams often present a wealth of information and creative solutions, so it's a good idea to examine them. The first step is usually to write them down upon waking; this is especially true if you believe you have had a prophetic dream, because seeing it in writing will help you have confidence in your ability to see what could happen. There are many wonderful Web sites, such as www.dreamtree.com, that can help you interpret and understand your dreams.

You can increase your ability to remember your dreams by taking a bath before bedtime with a mixture of the following, tied up in a piece of cheesecloth or pantyhose:

1 sprig of rosemary
2 carnations
¼ c. lavender buds
1 sprig of mint

As you soak in the tub, be sure to ask to remember the dreams that you'll have later that night. If there's a specific area of your life where you're looking for answers, perform the dream ritual on the night that it is most effective for the type of dream you're looking for:

Monday: prophetic dreams
Tuesday: sexual dreams
Wednesday: problem-solving dreams, dreams that strengthen
    the intellect
Thursday: money dreams
Friday: love dreams
Saturday: dreams to build patience and bring messages
    about habits you wish to break
Sunday: dreams to bring health, peace, and improvements
    to home life

Evelyn Smith-Herman had a desire to give to society but had no idea what she wanted to do. She took the required bath on a

Sunday and had a dream in which she was delivering something. She hoped she was not delivering pizza and took the bath again the following Sunday. She had another dream, but this time she was wrapping gifts. Now Evelyn has started a foundation that takes gifts to special needs children; she named it Angels Bearing Gifts. The first year she delivered twenty gifts; since then, she has found almost one hundred children who otherwise never would have celebrated their birthdays or Christmas. I'm honored to have helped Evelyn find her wonderful dream; for more information about Evelyn's foundation, visit the Web site, www.angels bearinggifts.com.

Another bedtime tradition can draw on the bounty of the earth to help stimulate your unconscious to help you find your path: hot cocoa. The ancient Aztecs believed that chocolate possesses magical properties; newlyweds ate it as an aphrodisiac, warriors used it to prepare for battle, and priests drank it to communicate with the gods. When you're at a crossroads and need to make a big decision, combine the following to call upon the magic of chocolate:

1 cup of boiling water
1 2-inch square of plain dark chocolate
⅛ tsp. powered cinnamon
⅛ tsp. vanilla
⅛ tsp. chili powder
Honey to taste

Sit quietly and sip the chocolate, asking the chocolate to stimulate your subconscious. Solutions will come as you sip.

The Magic Circle

The following ritual has led many clients to the paths they sought. It takes a lot of space and is most effective when you do it outside, where you can draw on the vital earth energy. Ideally you'll do it on a beach, where you can draw lines in the sand and feel the energy of a nearby body of water as well.

Exercise Your Spirit:	**Stand in Your Circle**
What you will need:	**Paper, 1 lodestone, 3 coins, a flashlight, and a stick (If you have trouble finding a lodestone, use a magnet instead.)**
Time:	**2 hours**

Before you go to the area that you will actually do this exercise,

- *Write a statement of what you want in each of the twelve houses, or areas, of your life:*

  First House: *The manner in which you project yourself; your self-image and awareness.*

  Example: *I am feeling very strong, confident and centered.*

Second House: *Money and possessions.*

> Example: *I am debt free and have $100,000 in the bank.*

Third House: *Communications and writing*

> Example: *My communication skills develop on all levels and in all areas with a tremendous heart and soul connection.*

Fourth House: *Home*

> Example: *My home is private, beautiful, warm, comfortable, and well designed with a lot of separate spaces such as a meditation area, gym, room for family and guests to stay and have privacy.*

Fifth House: *Children, romance, and creativity*

> Example: *I have a tremendously loving, growing relationship with my mate that heals our souls. My children are growing into happy, healthy adults with a close bond with their family and my mate and myself. My creativity is a source of income.*

Sixth House: Health, work

> Example: *I am very healthy and vibrant, happy and continuously improving my purification and vitality. I love the work that I do.*

Seventh House: *Marriage, relationships, partnerships, law*

Example: *I am married to a wonderful man who has a deep connection to me. Our relationship continues to grow and blossom throughout our lives on all levels. We are married in a beautiful island setting with close family and friends. I am creating partnerships that are trustworthy, honest and fun loving with talented people. I have learned from the past. I do not create entanglements that pull my emotional energy. I am free of legal entanglements.*

Eighth House: *Wealth of spouse, sex, trust, death*

Example: *My husband and I have an incredibly connected sex life as we continue to explore each other. My husband is a man who has allowed me to heal my trust issues. I am expanding in trust. My husband is very successful and very happy in what he does. Our wealth is put into doing great work, humanitarian work as well as providing for our loved ones.*

Ninth House: *Travel and higher education*

Example: *I am traveling with my husband all over the world. Our travels take us to many wonderful places where we meet many wonderful people. We travel for combined business and pleasure. We plan our trips and time away to allow for a lot of personal private time together and with our families. I finish my PhD program.*

Tenth House: *Career*

> Example: *I am recognized in business because of my conscious approach and humanitarian efforts in regard to employees and the running of my companies.*

Eleventh House: *Hopes and dreams, friends*

> Example: *My hopes and dreams continue to manifest. I attract and develop real friendships based on trust, honesty, mutual interest, love, and fun. My friendships are based on growth and challenge me. My mate is my best friend.*

Twelfth House: *Psychic abilities, spiritual service, karma, and meditation*

> Example: *My spiritual insight is continually growing and I listen to myself. I am connected to my intuition and I am guided by it. The light within me grows and guides me, and I release all my karma.*

Once you are at the location with your list completed,

- *Stand still and hold the lodestone on the seven main chakras of the body.*
- *Allow the lodestone to pull any energy that is holding you back (patterns, thoughts, past actions) out of your body.*
- *When you feel the pulling of the energy stop, either throw the stone in the ocean or a moving body of water or bury it.*

- *Moving in a counterclockwise direction, draw a circle about five feet in diameter using your feet (if you're on the beach) or a stick (if you're on harder ground).*
- *As you move around your circle, think about how you will feel as your hopes and dreams manifest and your circle completes itself.*
- *Using either your left foot (in sand) or your stick (on the ground), cut the circle in half, calling in the male/female energies (yin/yang) by asking for the help of God/Goddess.*
- *Cut the circle into fourths, calling in the four directions or the four elements with our earlier chant:* The earth, the air, the water, the fire, return, return, return, return.
- *Cut each fourth into thirds, representing the mother/ father, child, and Holy Spirit.*
- *At this point you should have twelve sections. Beginning from the center of your circle, walk each of the lines, moving in a counterclockwise direction*
- *Return to the center of your circle and say the following prayer:* You, who are the source of all power, whose rays illuminate the whole world, illuminate also my heart so that it too can create my life.
- *Visualize the sun's rays streaming forth into the world, entering your own heart, and streaming out of your heart into the world.*
- *Step into the section that would be at one o'clock if your circle were a clock, and read aloud what you wrote about your First House. Close your eyes and*

visualize what it would look and feel like to have it a reality.

- *Walk in a counterclockwise direction, stepping into each house, reading your statement, and visualizing each outcome. In the Second House, bury the three coins.*
- *When you have performed the ritual in each of the twelve sections, return to the center and feel the completeness.*
- *Repeat the following, six times:* So be it!

After working the first six magic keys, Janice came to see me saying, "I just do not know what to do with myself. All of a sudden I feel like I am waking up from a long sleep. I see how easy it is to not read the news, to not feel what is going on in the world around me. It is just too painful. I know there are people starving. I don't know how I can do my part, or if I even have a part." By performing the ritual of standing in her circle, Janice found her mission in teaching children to read. She wrote letters to all her friends and asked them to donate books so that she had her own library. She went to schools in the inner city and began to read to children. Soon others joined her in her work. She tells me that her life has never felt so fulfilling or so full.

The gifts that come from standing in your circle and discovering your path involve far more than finding work. When you are on your path, you feel it in every aspect of your life. Joshua and his wife, Lindsay, did this ceremony with me and found their marriage started getting better and better. They had never really discussed their goals, so this ritual gave them an opportunity to focus their combined energy on creating the life they both wanted. Each time I see them, they now have a new story to tell me about how their circle is filling in.

You may have a clearer idea of what your destiny is than you did when you began this journey, or it may still be a mystery to you. Either way, be patient, and expect the unexpected. We can never know what the universe has in store for us. In addition to the men and women whose inspiring stories you've already read about in these pages, I've worked with clients who have gone from being alone to finding their true love, from doing legal work that gave them no joy to starting a pet store and spreading joy to many animal owners and their pets, from looking for acting work to starring in a top-rated TV series, from living with chronic pain to hiking every day in the hills. What they have in common is that they remained open to the possibility of discovering their magic in ways they had never dreamed of!

Once you are on your path, stay in touch with the magic that led you there and you will go far. Live in a loving way and believe in yourself. Thinking good thoughts about yourself is an important key to success; have faith in your abilities to accomplish anything that you set out to do. Surround yourself with positive reminders of how good you feel; always expect the best to come into your life. You must surround yourself with quality, orderliness, and beauty, and they'll naturally attract good influences. Do the best you can do, and then leave the rest in God's hands. Work toward your goal, but concentrate on the quality of the effort more than the results; when you leave the success of the effort to God's will, you're less likely to get bogged down by impatience, frustration, anxiety, anger, or other psychological handicaps.

Remember, as a magus you now know that it's your magic but that you are not in control of the universe. The magic you share has been entrusted to you to develop and give back. Your magical self will show you how you are meant to share it. Cherish your magic, listen to it, cultivate it, and have fun as you share it with love and good wishes. The universe will take care of the rest.

So be it!

EPILOGUE:

The Responsibility of a Magus

By now it's likely that you will have noticed the acceleration of your life—your physical life, your emotional life, and especially your spiritual life. You have tapped into your magic and are feeling a connection to the universe. You have tools to create change, and you feel your personal power. This does not mean that you are special. It means that you are unique and are more clearly aware of your uniqueness. You are not only moving forward, you are gaining depth, and your life is attaining the beauty, profundity, and power that only depth can provide.

You, dear reader, are now ready to be a magus—to cross that invisible line and allow your unconscious to teach you its timeless wisdom. The greatest magic is love, and it is love that you are sharing whenever you share of yourself. You need only remember that

1. You are powerful and strong enough to be gentle and vulnerable. *Al Ser Vulnerable, Me Vuelo Invincible.*

2. You do not need any protection from love. You can receive love without fear. The cost of giving is receiving!

3. You must be totally honest with yourself. You have both the passion to move forward in your life and the compassion to be empathetic. That means that you can be compassionate with those who are still growing and learning. You will teach only those who want to learn, and you will be loving to all others.

4. You are flexible enough to transmute and transform anything you want, to shift any reality. You now know how to disengage from the negative and engage with the positive. You celebrate the mystery of change. You no longer need to control life, and you are allowing magic to do its thing.

5. You know that the past need not repeat itself. You are a transformer! You remember to be humble enough not to take anything for granted. You know that you are responsible for creating your reality. You focus on the solution, not the problem.

6. You are the creator of light, hope, dreams, and visions, and you know that you support them with the love and courage to let them come true. You never dream something without also creating the opportunity to manifest it. You know with certainty that your dreams will become your reality.

7. You value your spirituality and your magic enough to make them your highest priority. When you make your

spirit your priority, then everything else serves it—relationships, children, work, everything.

Exercise Your Spirit: **A Return to the Holy**
What you will need: **You and your wand**
Time: **20 minutes**

- *Reach below, then sweep both arms outward and say*

  Magic

- *Draw both arms downward, passing your hand over
  your body, and say*

  Love

- *Extend your left arm until it is perpendicular with
  your body, the palm upward as if cupping a ball,
  and say*

  My comrades beside me

- *Extend your right arm until it is perpendicular with
  your body, the palm upward as if cupping a ball,
  and say*

  My angels over me

- *Bring your hands together at your heart, one hand
  cupping the other, and say*

  We are all one.

- *Flatten your hands upon your heart, then pick up your wand and move it above your head, under your feet.*
- *Place your wand down on the earth. Pick it up and walk to a mirror. Point the wand at your image in the mirror and say*

You are a magus.

The life you ordered has arrived! You are creating your future right now, so walk into your future with love and magic to share with all. So be it! And so it is. *AMEN!*

REFERENCE LIST

Books that have influenced my work:

Andresine, Jensine (editor). *Cognitive Models and Spiritual Maps.* Imprint Academic, Charlottesville, VA, 2000.

Bardon, Franz. *Initiation into Hermetics.* Osiris-Verlag, West Germany, 1962.

Blofeld, John. *The Book of Change.* George Allen & Unwin, London, 1968.

Brown, Dan. *The Da Vinci Code.* Doubleday, New York, 2003.

Campbell, Joseph. *The Hero with a Thousand Faces.* Princeton University Press, Princeton, NJ, 1972.

Dyer, Wayne. *The Sky's the Limit.* Pocket Books, New York, 1981.

Elgin, Duane. *Awakening Earth.* William Morrow, New York, 1993.

Foundation for Inner Peace. *A Course in Miracles.* Foundation for Inner Peace, Tiburon, CA, 1975.

Gawain, Shakti. *Creative Visualization.* New World Library, Novato, CA, 2002 (25th Anniversary Edition).

Hodson, Geoffrey. *The Call to the Heights*. Quest Books, Wheaton, IL, 1975.

Jampolsky, Gerald, MD. *Love is Letting Go of Fear*. Ten Speed Press, Berkeley, CA, 2004 (25th Anniversary Edition).

Kilner, W. J. *The Human Aura*. Citadel, New York, 1920.

Knight, Gareth. *A Practical Guide to Qabalistic Symbolism*. Vol 2. Helios Book Service, Cheltenham, 1965.

Kübler-Ross, Elisabeth. *On Death and Dying*. Scribner, New York, 1969.

Lamsa, George (translator). *The Holy Bible*.

Leadbeater, C. W. *The Hidden Side of Christian Festivals*. St. Albans Press, London, 1920.

Levine, Stephen. *Who Dies?* Anchor Books, New York, 1989.

Levry, Joseph Michael. *The Divine Doctor*. Rootlight, New York, 2003.

Myss, Caroline. *Anatomy of the Spirit*. Harmony Books, New York, 1996.

Osho. *The Rebel*. Hind Pocket Books, Delhi, 2000.

Ram Dass, Baba. *Be Here Now*. Lama Foundation, San Cristobal, NM, 1971.

Regardie, Israel. *The Golden Dawn. 4 Vols*. Llewellyn Publications, St. Paul, MN, 1971.

Scovel-Shinn, Florence. *The Game of Life*. DeVorss & Co, Camarillo, CA, 1925.

Starbird, Margaret. *The Woman with the Alabaster Jar*. Bear & Company, Rochester, Vermont 1993.